# GREEN
# WITCHCRAFT

# GREEN WITCHCRAFT

## A Practical Guide to Discovering the Magic of Plants, Herbs, Crystals, and Beyond

Paige Vanderbeck

Illustrations by Studio Muti

ROCKRIDGE PRESS

Interior and Cover Designer: Erik Jacobsen
Art Producer: Hillary Frileck
Editor: Sean Newcott
Production Editor: Mia Moran
Illustrations © 2019 Studio Muti. NASA/Bill Dunford, p. 96

ISBN: Print 978-1-64611-564-8 | eBook 978-1-64611-565-5
R0

*Dedicated to Jimmy Hoppa—RIP my lucky moon rabbit.*

# Contents

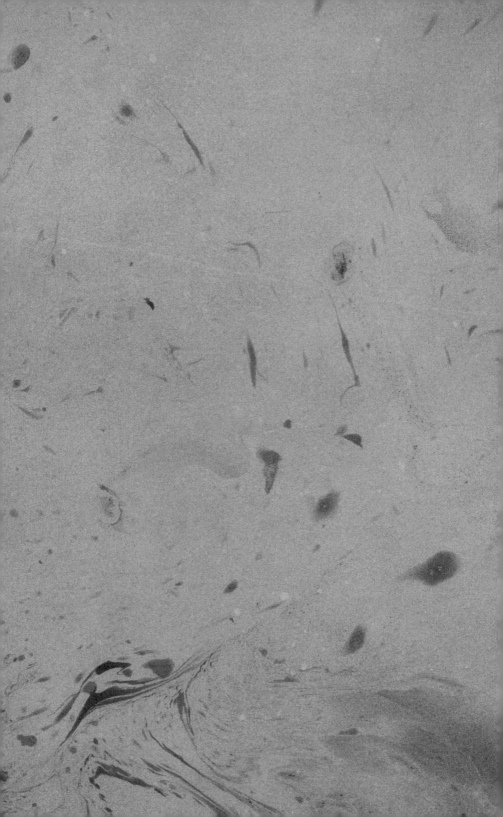

# Introduction

I felt the call of the earth from a young age. I couldn't keep my toes out of the mud, and I ate any fruit or vegetable right off the plant. I climbed trees (usually to get to the cherries or crab apples), made friends with the neighborhood animals, and raised tadpoles into frogs in an old claw-foot tub in the backyard. Living in the middle of the automotive capital of Canada, I would lie in the grass watching the city buses go by, dreaming about the day I, too, could be trusted to take this Chariot of the Teenage Gods to school. I share this because there's this myth that everyone who loves or connects with the earth lives on a farm or in the middle of the woods, but that isn't true. Anyone can develop a relationship with the earth, regardless of what part of it they currently happen to be standing on.

One of the first things I learned about real witchcraft was that it was a path for those who wanted to live in harmony with the earth—those who wanted to grow and harvest plants for magic and medicine, and to honor the spirits of the trees, the animals, and even the rocks around them. I knew right away I'd found the path I was meant to walk.

If you've found your way to this book, I imagine you've felt that same call from the earth: to slow down and listen to what it has to teach you. Maybe you've always had an incredible green thumb or have always wanted to learn to use natural medicine, or maybe you've recently realized you need to make a more meaningful spiritual connection with the earth.

*Green Witchcraft* is a guide to creating a relationship with all things natural and supernatural and for harnessing that energy in a way that can affect your everyday life. Many of the plants, flowers, stones, and more that you'll find in this book have ancient origins—both medicinal and mystical—but all the exercises are designed to work in the modern world.

# PART I

# Understanding Green Witchcraft

I n part 1 of this book, we'll cover everything you need to know before embarking on the path of green witchcraft, including some history, values and beliefs, the necessary tools, and making your space ready to work with plants and stones. I'll explain what words like "magic" and "energy" actually mean to witches, and some of the myths and misconceptions about magic and the people who believe in it.

### Chapter One

# The Way of the Green Witch

This chapter delves into the philosophies
and practices that define green witchcraft
and those who practice it, as well as its
origins and focus on the natural world.

# The Green Witchcraft Tradition

Green witchcraft is a practice and a lifestyle. It's also a relationship between you and the earth. The earth supports you, provides for you, and heals you, and you respond in kind. The more you put into your relationship with the earth, the more you get out of it. By studying and working with natural elements like plants, weather, crystals, and the cosmos, witches become in tune with the cycles of growth, evolution, harmony, life, and death. The wisdom of the earth is infinite, and so, too, is the learning process in which witches revel.

In researching witchcraft, you might find information about established traditions or even religions that incorporate the practice into their belief systems. The most popular witchcraft-based religion is called Wicca and is covered beginning on page 4 of this book. On its own, however, the practice of green witchcraft is not a religion. This path is open to people of all religions and cultural backgrounds. It can be practiced in tandem with any religion of your choosing or on its own as a spiritual practice.

If you're still unsure if green witchcraft is for you because you don't fit the image of a witch you have in your head, go ahead and give your head a shake because here's the truth—anyone can be a witch. I know that's a loaded word and may even scare you, so let's dispel some of myths and misconceptions about green witches.

## "I can't be a green witch because . . . "

⌀ **"I like living in the city, working in an office building, and wearing makeup and high heels or a suit."** Witches have come a long way since the days of Hansel and Gretel in the deep, dark woods. People from all walks of life, from all backgrounds, and with all sorts of interests have found their way to witchcraft and magic because they form a spiritual path that lets them make the rules about their own lives.

🖋 **"I believe in science and Western medicine."** Believing in the power of nature and believing in the power of humanity are not mutually exclusive. You can protect yourself with both vaccines and a sprig of rue hung above your front door.

🖋 **"I have the opposite of a green thumb. I kill everything."** This one is so common. There are so many different ways of working with plants, and growing them yourself is only one of those ways. We all have different skills. Maybe you kill every plant you bring home but draw the most beautiful renderings of living plants you encounter, or run an organization that works to fight climate change.

🖋 **"I'm a faithful Christian, and I was taught that witchcraft is evil."** Witchcraft and magic are not evil, and the vast majority of modern witches you meet are not satanic or even anti-Christian. It may surprise you to know that Christian witches exist. There are also Jewish, Muslim, and atheist witches. If your religion enriches your life and provides you with comfort and understanding about the world, there's no reason to give it up or to think that witchcraft contradicts it.

🖋 **"Only women can be witches."** This one is, without a doubt, my least favorite misconception about witches out there. Anyone can be a witch. There is no one set of rules about who can be a witch or how you have to look, dress, or love.

Since green witchcraft is not a religion or tradition on its own, there's no initiation process or main governing body to put you on your path. That doesn't mean, however, that there's no one for you to learn from. The everyday uses, chemical composition, and growing cycles of plants and minerals are just as important to understand as their magical uses and energies. You can enroll in courses that teach herbalism, botany, geology, traditional Chinese medicine, and agriculture at many colleges and universities around the world, or you can join a local community garden or wild-crafting group. Starting on page 161, I've provided a list of resources, including books and websites, that can help you learn both the magical and mundane secrets of natural magic.

## Spirituality & Witchcraft

The most popular Western religion that includes the practice of witchcraft is called Wicca, a modern religion created in the 1940s in England by a man named Gerald Gardner and shared with the wider public in the 1950s. Many of the concepts and structure of modern witch practices come from Gardner and his first coven. Wicca is an open-minded religion with positive views about sexuality and women's rights, and focuses heavily on communion with and service of the earth. Instead of worshipping one god, Wiccans usually worship a god and goddess or even many gods and goddesses. Since Wicca's inception, the number of people practicing it or simply finding their spiritual path through witchcraft has grown exponentially. Currently, witchcraft is the fastest-growing spiritual movement in North America.

Spirituality, like witchcraft, is a big part of many religions but is not a religion in and of itself. It's more of a mindset. Spiritual people tend to understand that we, as humans, do not know everything and that one of the reasons we are all here is to seek out answers to questions, even those that may seem impossible to answer. Religion is one way in which many people scratch their spiritual itch, but it's not the only way.

# Finding Your Path

Spirituality takes many paths. Those who find their way to green witchcraft typically feel a strong connection to the natural world. They may feel most at peace in the woods or by a body of water, may enjoy tending to a garden, or may consider themselves animal lovers or environmentalists. They understand that they—and everything they see—are deeply connected to the earth on which they walk. For those who are spiritually inclined, the path of green witchcraft may call to them in a million different ways, if they are listening and looking for an invitation, from falling leaves during meditation to the surprisingly medicinal weed growing in their front lawns to the sound of the wind rushing past leaves, whispering magical sounds. The natural world speaks to us in subtle yet powerful ways.

For those who are curious about green witchcraft or new to the craft, resources for honing their inclinations are plentiful. The Internet puts a giant repository of information just a few clicks away. A local library or bookstore can help you discover books like this one. And local metaphysical stores sometimes offer classes as well as ways for people to meet others on the same spiritual path. For those who prefer to learn on their own, the natural world is replete with all the tools and materials needed to create healing and magic through the use of some independent research and intuition. Once you make up your mind to follow the path of the green witch, a plush green carpet will unfurl at your feet.

# Green Witchcraft through the Ages

"Witch" can be a pretty loaded word. Throughout time, people who called themselves witches, and even some who didn't, were put on trial and executed as blasphemers and heretics. It's no surprise that so many chose to go by other names instead, like "midwife," "wise man or woman," "healer," "herbalist," "shaman," "apothecary," or "medicine man or woman." In some places and times, there wasn't even a word for "witch" because what we now call folk magic was just another common household practice. These are the spiritual and historical ancestors of the modern green witch. Though practices vary widely across the world, all these healers studied local plants and foods and their effects on the body, mind, and spirit, and could often be sought out for spiritual counsel. By learning about these ancestors, green witches come to develop a sense of their place in a long line of people who have harnessed the power of the earth to heal the body, mind, and soul. Today, the most similar paths to green witchcraft are kitchen and hedge witchcraft. All three share a connection to the earth and focus on using elements from the natural world for healing. While green witches are the most connected to plants, kitchen witches incorporate anything available in the home into their practice, and hedge witches may incorporate dream and astral journeying into their arsenal of tools.

Though witchcraft and science may seem to be at odds, many who walk a green path have found that technology is an excellent tool for getting in touch with the natural world. You can use technology to keep a journal of your work with plants, identify flora and fauna in the wild, and access several years' worth of research with the click of a button. Green technology, like solar and wind power, can connect you with the energy of the earth while working to protect the environment, and that, to me, is magic.

# Acts of Magic

Magic is the art of creating change in ourselves and in our lives through acts of intention and a spiritual connection with all things natural and supernatural. This magic is not illusory. It's meant not to trick anyone but rather to provide another way of looking at the world.

Magic is about harnessing the natural energy that's all around us and within us. Instead of powering the lights, magic powers our dreams and aspirations. It's the energy of imagination, inspiration, and intuition. Instead of running that power through a wire or a light bulb, we run it through our hands, minds, and hearts by casting spells.

If you paid attention in science class, you know that everything in existence is made of energy and that it can never be truly created or destroyed, only recycled. When you use magic, you are directing the re-formation, or recycling, of available energy for a specific purpose. Sometimes when a spell doesn't work, it's because the energy needed wasn't available. This is where the idea of sacrifice comes in. By offering something, you're making its energy available, and the more energy we put in, the more we get back. Since our thoughts, words, feelings, and actions are all energy, sacrifices can take the form of a song or dance. Since matter is made up of energy, some food you've prepared, herbs you've gathered or grown, or even a stick of incense you light can serve as a sacrifice. While these things may seem mundane, intention can turn them into tools of your magic practice.

# Finding Harmony through Green Witchcraft

If you're reading this book, you probably already feel a strong connection to nature. Practicing green witchcraft is about creating a harmonious relationship with the earth and, therefore, all the creatures with which we share this planet. All of us have some sort of relationship with the earth because we need it to survive, but in a healthy and harmonious relationship, both sides give and take equally; in other words, both sides provide support and are therefore supported. They don't just exist in close proximity to each other but instead are a fundamental part of each other's lives. When we live in harmony with the earth, we are on one hand supported, aided, and needed, and on the other hand, we need, aid, and support the earth.

This relationship with the earth is something that makes walking the green path unique, because it means we are always connected to the energy of the natural world. You don't have to live in a cottage in the middle of a dense forest to cultivate this relationship. When you learn to live in harmony with the earth, every space becomes a sacred space. Whether you live in a concrete jungle in an apartment with a small balcony, or on a sprawling nature preserve, the earth is there for you. In a world where balance is sometimes difficult to come by, finding harmony with the earth offers a foundation for healing and magic to take place.

## Standards & Values

Since there's no one single green witchcraft tradition and it's not a religion with its own rules, there's no standard of ethics for this practice. However, because green witches have such a strong connection to the earth and its cycles and inhabitants, values such as sustainability, ethical food consumption, animal rights, and environmentalism often come up. Some green witches focus their magical efforts on healing the planet and reversing global warming, while others stop at recycling or volunteering for different eco-friendly causes. I've met many green witches who follow a vegetarian or vegan diet as part of their spiritual practice and others who say prayers of gratitude to the spirits of the animals they consume. Once you learn how the earth communicates with you, it'll tell you what it needs.

## Healing the Self & Others

In green witchcraft, healing is both a core principle and a type of magic. Working with natural allies, like plants and minerals, has always been about healing to facilitate growth, as you learned earlier, but it goes a little bit deeper than that. There's a difference between healing an illness and treating it. Western medicine is very focused on treating the symptoms of illness. This is so important, but it isn't the same as healing the illness. Let's say you're suffering from insomnia and you go to your doctor. You could leave with a prescription for a sleep aid or, if you visit a holistic doctor, maybe a box of chamomile tea with valerian root to help you fall asleep. This solves the problem of being too tired to function, but doesn't address what caused you to get to that point. Just as you might decide to see a counselor if you feel your insomnia may be stress related, green witchcraft aims to address the underlying issue, not simply the symptom. Some possible solutions include sleeping with a piece of citrine, hanging a dream catcher in your window if you're being plagued by nightmares, and burning sage and lavender in your bedroom to clear any disruptive energy.

Green witchcraft gives you the tools to create a more holistic plan for healing that can be applied to illness, personal relationships, your home, your career, and even the whole planet if you see fit. Sharing these tools or your skills with others is also a type of healing, for you and them. Being of service to other beings on the planet in this way transforms a lot of those parts of yourself, which seem so broken, into a power you can use to create real change.

# Communing with the Natural World

There is no better teacher in the study of green witchcraft than the natural world, with all of its ancient wisdom. Long before the age of enlightenment, when the scientific method began to take shape, humans read the earth and stars like an instruction manual. They watched the sky for important messages that informed their lives, such as when to start growing, when to fish or hunt, when to stay inside, what direction to travel in, or what kind of actions they could take to improve the lives of their people. Witches understand that just because humans stopped receiving those messages doesn't mean they are not being sent. The following are some of the ways in which the earth is communicating with us and how we can learn to listen.

**The Elements:** These are not the chemical compounds from the periodic table, but like those, they make up the universe. The Western elements are earth, air, fire, water, and spirit (or aether or ether). Many witches feel it's important to bring in the energy of all the elements when performing acts of magic, or to focus on one specifically that can lend the right kind of energy. For example, water energy is very emotional, so it's perfect in rituals concerning love and relationships. It can be incorporated into magic in the form of blessed water, aquatic plants, or a magical bath.

**The Sun, Moon & Stars:** Just as natural as anything occurring in nature here on the planet, the cosmos is constantly speaking to those prepared to listen, and there are so many ways to do that. Not only is our entire concept of time based on the movements and habits of the celestial bodies, but by studying astrology you can also gain deeper knowledge about human behavior and history. The moon phases put us in touch with emotional changes and seasons and even further our insight into humanity. Paying attention to the movement of the sun in your area can teach you everything from navigation to the growing cycles of plants and animals.

**Weather:** I truly hate that talking about the weather is considered meaningless small talk, because I could talk about it all day. The weather can tell you so much about a place or season and can even indicate when something is very wrong. In stories, the weather often reflects the feelings of the characters or the events unfolding in the plot; but in real life, it's often the other way around. Weather can show us our possibilities and limitations and dictate when and how we undertake tasks.

**Plants & Flowers:** Plants and flowers are constantly sending us messages with their scent, shape, color, growing cycles, flavor, and even the animals they attract or repel. Plants can save lives, and plants can take them just as quickly. They can bless us with abundance or curse us with poverty and starvation. They can also be friends and support systems, sources of inspiration, and a language we use to communicate with others.

**Animals:** Having a close, emotional, and respectful relationship with animals is a big part of my personal practice, and I know I'm not alone. Not only can local animals teach us about the natural cycles of nature, but they can also teach us about the supernatural, magic, and all things unseen. Animals are instinctual and very psychic and can sense changes in energy, sudden moments of danger, and even spirits

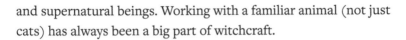

and supernatural beings. Working with a familiar animal (not just cats) has always been a big part of witchcraft.

**Food:** This might tie into your relationships with animals and plants, or it might not. Either way, our relationship with food is very significant, personal, and often cultural. Many witches apply mindful and intuitive behaviors to their dietary choices and needs, using food to maintain a connection with their body. For a lot of people, food can also form a strong connection to their local environment or ancestral heritage.

**Minerals & Crystals:** Not only can naturally occurring minerals and crystals vary widely from place to place, but because they're so ancient, they also connect us across time and space. None of the smart technology that connects us all would be possible without quartz. That's why minerals and crystals are often called things like elders or record keepers.

**The Earth:** It may seem obvious, but if you want to commune with the earth, try saying "hello." Sometimes it's as simple as sitting outside, opening your heart and mind, and waiting for a reply.

# Worldly Witchcraft

Don't be surprised if your practice changes if you move or travel to a new location, even within your own country or region. My city is situated along the path of the Underground Railroad, so hoodoo practitioners are plentiful, but two hours away in London, Ontario, which is known for its forests, Druidic practitioners who worship trees are more common. The magic of Salem, Massachusetts, is inspired by English practices from colonial times because of its infamous witch trials in 1692. In Louisiana, slaves and free people of color combined their traditional African religious practices with Christian saints and rituals to avoid persecution, and this became New Orleans voodoo. In New York, you can travel to the village of Lily Dale, the birthplace of spiritism, which is completely inhabited by psychics and mediums. Magical practices are influenced by local cultures, climates, plants, environment, and even laws. Always be open to learn about and explore your natural environment and the kinds of magical energy you can find there.

# Green Heroes

Though it's not necessary to worship any gods or goddesses to practice green witchcraft, personifying the unknown is something that has always brought comfort and understanding to humans. Many ancient gods helped explain the way things worked: The sun rose because of the sun god, the land was created by the volcano goddess, and even the earth itself was a goddess of life and abundance. These stories can still serve as inspiration and a reminder that, at one time, magic was just a part of life.

Mother Nature is just that—the personification of the earth and the forces of nature. I'm sure you've cursed her under your breath during a sudden storm once or twice. There are goddesses associated with the moon in almost every ancient culture and religion in the world. The moon has so much pull here on earth (literally) that it's difficult to ignore. Faeries too represent elemental energy and are closely aligned with nature. In some legends, faeries are actually nature spirits or demigods themselves. Many witches build faery houses in their gardens to attract and appease these nature spirits, and some leave offerings in the hope they'll help plants flourish.

## Chapter Two
# Harnessing the Powers of the Green Witch

Now that you know the magical and emotional motivations behind green witchcraft, it's time to gather tools and set up a space appropriate for making magic.

# The Curious Witch

Thinking that you know everything is probably one of the worst curses you can cast on yourself. Curiosity is one of the greatest gifts in the world, and it is vital to the practice of green witchcraft. There is always more for you to learn and even some things not yet discovered. The second you deny it, all of that is lost to you. A good green witch is always open to new information, always willing to dedicate time and energy to their craft, and humble enough to defer to those with more experience. Over time, you'll gain wisdom, but you still will never know everything. Trust your own experiences with nature and the experiences of those who have something to teach you. This will ensure that your practice is always growing. If you need another reason, some plants and minerals are toxic, some environments are dangerous, and pride really can cost you your life. Being willing to slow down and learn, rather than rush in and show off, will be much more fulfilling in the long run.

# Finding Your Center

The energy of the earth is the energy of life itself, which is why green witchcraft is a spiritual practice centered on practical activities and tools available in your everyday life. This brand of witchery takes inspiration and energy from the world around you that you can use to create a happy and harmonious life. There are no limits on what you can create and accomplish with magic, but it's best to start with the basics. The following are seven of the many branches on the tree of life, where magic can spark growth and transformation.

- *Abundance:* On this branch, we have our jobs and career goals, our relationship with money, and our ability to amass the things we want and need to be happy. It's also where we find the ways we show gratitude and what we share with others.

- *Happiness:* Here, we find the things that make us happy, of course, but more so, it's how we find happiness. Sometimes the magic that will make you the happiest will be about letting go and moving on.

- *Harmony:* This branch is large but coexists perfectly with all the others. This is where our relationships blossom and grow, our needs are supported, and we learn the ways we fit into the world.

- *Health:* This branch is where we care for ourselves and others. It's where we find our energy, sustenance, and beauty. With magic, we can heal ourselves and others, body and soul.

- *Love:* This branch is bursting with flowers and fruits that attract all the creatures of the planet. Here is where we nurture our relationships with others and the one we have with ourselves.

- *Protection:* Here is where we deal with our home, our aura, our security, and our strength. It's where we conquer our fears and safeguard the things we've built and people we love.

- *Wisdom:* This is the branch of knowledge and enlightenment. Life is a learning experience, and magic can help us open ourselves to the wisdom of the earth and foster a deep sense of inner peace.

As you continue along the green path, you may find that your own tree has more branches or maybe fewer. You may find that you're particularly skilled at some kinds of magic, and that branch will become larger than the others. Never limit yourself. There are so many different kinds of magic and ways to practice out there, but if you begin with these seven, your life will be flourishing before long.

# Helpful Tools for a Green Practice

When creating your green witch toolkit, it's important to remember that this is a practical path of your own design. There's no official list of tools for your altar or workspace, no must-have herbs, and no "can't live without them" crystals. The kinds of tools you need will depend on how you intend to practice, but these are the ones I use every day to connect with and study the earth.

- **Herbs & Greens:** Herbs are small, leafy, seed-bearing plants without a woody stem. They also die back after the growing season. They're mostly used in cooking, medicine, and perfume because they're usually flavorful and have a nice, strong smell. Some common ones are basil, rosemary, and lemongrass.

- **Plants & Flowers:** You can also choose to work with trees, houseplants, fruit- and vegetable-bearing plants, and flowers. There is a flower for every branch of magic, whether you're looking to attract love (rose), get rich (honeysuckle), or open your third eye to the psychic world (Datura).

- **Stones & Crystals:** In the world of mineral magic, the crystal is king, and it's easy to see why. Crystals are natural minerals like rocks, but they're colorful and sparkly and have patterns that mimic the natural forces of nature. Stones, on the other hand, are the pristine single minerals in their original form. Both of these can be used in magic to connect you to the earth (aragonite), direct energy for specific purposes (quartz), absorb energy from yourself or the space around you (obsidian), and wear on your body for healing (amethyst).

- **Notebook/Journal:** Casting spells, especially in the beginning, will feel a lot like a science experiment. You'll want to make note of the tools and method you used, the environmental and cosmic conditions on the day you cast the spell, how it felt at the time, and, eventually, the results. You can take notes digitally or by hand or use both methods. Include drawings and sketches, personal journal entries, and reference information on the plants and minerals you use most. It's your green grimoire.

- **Fireproof Dish, Matches & Charcoal Discs:** Incense can come in many different forms, like sticks and cones, as well as loose blends of herbs and resins that get burned on a charcoal disc. You can find fireproof dishes made of cast iron, ceramic, brass, and copper in the shape of a classic cauldron. Pick one that you really like. Charcoal discs can be bought in packs of 10 and are best lit with a wooden match. I also like to keep some sand in the bottom to cradle the charcoal disc and absorb the heat.

- **Mortar & Pestle:** The mortar and pestle are used to grind herbs and resins to make powders, incense blends, or medicines. I recommend having one made of a heavy material, like granite, for herbs and a second one made of a smoother material for resins or minerals. Metal won't trap the resins, so it's easier to keep clean.

- **Knives & Scissors:** Most witches keep separate knives and scissors for magical plants and other purposes, but that depends on you. Kitchen witches who work with culinary herbs and magical food have a single pair of scissors. Make sure these are kept sharp and clean and that the blade always matches the job you're doing.

- **Mason Jars & Glass Bowls:** Witches were obsessed with mason jars before they were cool. These are used to store your plants and herbs as well as the things you create, like incense blends or bath salts. The bowls, of course, are for mixing. Glass won't absorb or affect the smell of your plants and herbs, and glass bowls can be cleaned and reused.

- **Natural Cotton:** This can be in the form of strips of cloth, small bags, string, or the fluffy batting used in pillows. It's breathable, allowing for the free flow of energy.

- **Candles:** As the main representation of the fire element, candles are very popular in witchcraft. Candles can be carved, dressed in oils and herbs, and burned for specific purposes according to the color of the wax.

- **Essential & Carrier Oils:** Essential oils are extremely concentrated oils made from individual plants or flowers that have medicinal or magical properties and smell like the real thing. They're not safe to use directly, so they're blended with what's called a carrier oil that is skin safe and has a bit of scent of its own, like olive, jojoba, or avocado oil.

- **Rope or Twine:** These can be used to tie bundles of herbs for hanging or burning and can also be used in knotwork spells for attraction, banishing, and protection. Hemp is a great material for rope or twine because the plant is a magical amplifier, as you'll learn in chapter 5.

- **Broom:** Yes, witches really do use brooms. Unfortunately, no one's figured out a spell for flying yet, but we'll get there. The broom is used for physical and magical cleaning and serves as a home protection charm when kept by the front door.

- **Divinatory Tools:** Divination is what we used to call fortune-telling, receiving messages from spirits, gods, or the unseen. Tarot and oracle cards, pendulums, and crystal balls are all divinatory tools. You can also get more earth-based tools like crystal runes or Celtic Ogham staves, which are carved into sacred wood.

- **The Hands:** Your hands have a tremendous amount of power. They have the ability to create and destroy and to give and receive. You'll use your hands to receive energy from natural tools like crystals and to send that energy out armed with your intention. You'll be sticking your hands in the earth, using them to harvest flowers and thorns and to move energy, so it's important to keep them healthy and clean. The herbal healing salve in chapter 6 is great for garden-worn hands and harnesses the energy of seven magical herbs and plants.

# The World Tree

For as long as human beings have been sharing spiritual stories, trees have played a leading role. Almost every culture has a world tree, or sacred tree, that unites all the life on earth with that of the heavens and the creatures of the underworld. The world tree reminds us that magic is never far away, and when we need it, we need only reach up to the stars and root ourselves down into the earth like a great tree. In the Garden of Eden of the Bible and the Garden of the Hesperides of Greek mythology, the apple tree was sacred, bestowing knowledge and wisdom on whomever ate the fruit. The world tree in Norse legend was a gigantic ash named Yggdrasil, and its mighty branches supported a hanging Odin in a sacrifice to himself. The Druids of the British Isles consider the oak sacred and use the shelter of large oak groves for magical gatherings. In India, the Buddha attained enlightenment while sitting under a sacred fig known as Sri Maha Bodhi. Though the Bodhi tree has died or been felled by storms, a new one always grows in its place. You'll meet all of these magical trees in chapter 7, "The Wisdom of Wood."

# Creating a Green Space

Your home is your sanctuary, and when you practice green witch-craft, this is doubly true. Your home can serve as a place of power and source of magical energy, helping you along your path. Now that you've got all of your physical tools, it's time to create the right energy around the home.

Cleaning out and creating a space dedicated to your practice makes it clear that you are working to create the space in your life for spirituality. It doesn't have to be an entire room or a green-house, though it can be. Set up your tools and any magical plants or crystals you have. Make sure you have a flat workspace and a little bit of storage. Once you have your dedicated area, it's time to move on to the rest of the house. You want to have a fresh start on this new path, with a soothing and tranquil space to welcome in the new.

# Elements in the Home

That workspace you created will also serve as your altar or shrine, a place through which to channel energy, honor heroes and spirits, and connect to the elements. My altar serves as both a workspace and a source of inspiration. This is especially important for city witches like me who might struggle to have constant contact with all of the elements on a day-to-day basis, but everyone can bene-fit from having this witchy oasis in their home. Start by gathering items or images that represent the elements to you. Earth can be represented with plants, crystals, sand, salt, and wood. The smoke coming from your incense can represent air, or you can use images of birds and naturally shed feathers. Water can be incorporated easily with a glass of fresh water, but you can also set up a small

# ENERGETIC CLEANING

Cleaning out energetic debris, or stale energy that hasn't moved, could include lingering feelings about a breakup or even spiritual energy that was in your home before you moved in. You can clear energy using smoke, sound, movement, magical waters, and help from minerals and crystals. The idea is to fill the space with a positive energy so there's no room for negativity to linger.

Sound waves bounce from surface to surface, knocking old, stagnant energy out of its hiding places. Music is also just good for the soul. You can use a bell, a Tibetan singing bowl, or even a playlist of your absolute favorite songs—ones that always make you smile.

Smoke is the most popular way of clearing space, both in homes and in personal energy fields. Herbs for cleansing, protection, and blessing are burned on charcoal discs or in bundles, with sage being the most popular. You'll learn how to make a smoke bundle with sacred plants for this purpose in chapter 5.

Gather your herbs, a fireproof bowl, and matches or a lighter on your new workspace. Before you start, set an intention. What do you want your home to feel like? Hold that in your mind. Wave the smoke around the furniture and along the walls. Make sure smoke gets under furniture, in corners and closets, and anywhere dust and stale energy might collect. Move through the whole house until you get to the front door (or an appropriate window if you live in an apartment building), and as you open it, watch the smoke carry all of that excess energy out of your home and life.

water feature or aquarium. I have a dried starfish and seashells from both the Atlantic and Pacific Oceans on my altar for water. Candles are my favorite representation of fire, but you can also use volcanic rock or dried chile peppers.

In the Chinese practice of feng shui, different areas of the home are ruled by specific elements. To keep the energy of their home balanced, feng shui practitioners place their shrine at the center of the home, sometimes known as the hearth or heart, and make sure all elements are represented.

# The Sacred Outdoors

If you're fortunate enough to have a yard where you can do gardening and landscaping, practicing outdoors can be very easy. You can build an outdoor altar or shrine, plant a witch's garden and trees with sacred energy, and maybe even incorporate composting and sustainable energy to tend to your relationship with the planet. For many of us, this is just a beautiful dream, but that doesn't mean that an active connection with nature is out of reach. As we learned earlier, when you learn to live in harmony with the earth, every space becomes a sacred space.

The most important plants, herbs, and flowers for you to learn about are the ones that grow locally. What kinds of trees grow where you live? What are the native flower species? Are there poisonous plants and fungi onto which you might stumble? Their energy is all around you, and you have the privilege to be able to interact with them at all stages of growth, learning exactly how they work.

When you're in public natural spaces like parks, trails, and beaches, it's important to be respectful of the other people around you and of the environment. A good guide here is to "take only pictures and leave only footprints." You don't want to cause damage in the name of your spiritual pursuits. This isn't the place for rituals that include burning candles or incense or that require the use of a lot of different tools and materials. You can create a travel altar or shrine using a small box and adding in elemental symbols, some salt or sage for purification, a multipurpose crystal like clear quartz, and maybe your tarot cards or runes. Keep it simple, design any rituals to fit the space, and work with the energy of the natural environment.

## A Witch's Garden

No matter where you live or what kinds of plants are natural to your area, you can have your own witch's garden. Even as a beginner with a small amount of space, you can grow amazing herbs for cooking, medicine, and magic. If you're just getting started, pick one plant ally that matches your space and level of experience or one that focuses on a particular branch of magic with which you want to work. Take the time to learn your plant's needs, its likes and dislikes, and the perfect spot for it to live. Treat your plant to the energy of love and care, and it will respond in kind. When you harvest any part of your plant for use in magic, take a moment to express your gratitude. Once you've got the care and use of your magical plant figured out, feel free to bring more into the family and repeat the process.

A larger witch garden will require some planning before you begin. Start by selecting a spot for your garden and note how much light—solar and lunar—and rain it gets on a regular basis as well as what kinds of animals call it home. Cleanse the space energetically with smoke like you did in your house, or plant six quartz crystals in a circle around your future garden. The really exciting part is planning the makeup of your witch's garden. You can select

# FULL MOON ON THE BEACH

The moon is closely tied to the element of water and the ocean tides. On the night of the full moon, gather your travel altar, a bottle of water to drink, a mason jar, and a blanket to sit on. Pick a spot illuminated by the moon, where you can sit undisturbed. Take your altar items and bottle of water and lay them out on the blanket before you, where they can soak up the moonlight. This is a simple way of cleansing spiritual items and charging them with the magical energy of the moon. Look out over the water and breathe in time with the waves rolling in. Feel the moonlight surround your whole body, and imagine breathing it into your lungs, belly, and heart. Imagine that same light filling your altar tools and bottle of water. Stay as long as you like. Before you leave, fill your mason jar with that moon-charged natural water. If it's saltwater, pour it across the threshold of your home for cleansing. If it's freshwater, use it to water your plants and pass that lunar energy onto them. You can drink your bottle of moon water or add it to a magical bath when you get home.

plants that all have a specific energy or purpose, like abundance or love. Psychic witches may choose to plant a moon garden filled with night-blooming flowers and plants that increase intuition and psychic energy. Those with a desire to heal can focus on medicinal plants. The kitchen witch might choose to grow fruits, vegetables, and culinary herbs to infuse all the meals they make with magical intent. Make sure whatever you choose can share space and soil and will flourish under the conditions in your yard. If your yard is home to wild animals like rabbits, which may eat their way through your garden, it's okay to put up a fence, but it's good magical manners to leave a little bit behind for them.

A great source of information on what and when to plant in your area is an almanac, which you can get in booklet or digital format. You'll notice that the calendar makes note of moon and astrological phases; that's because the gravitational pull of the moon and the sign it's currently in can lend energy to your gardening efforts. For example, the first quarter phase, right after the new moon, is a favorable time to plant most aboveground crops like herbs. You can find a full guide to gardening by moon phases in chapter 5.

The plants you grow in your garden can be used in your spells and rituals and to make incenses, potions, teas, salves, and baths. Your garden also serves as a liminal space—a bridge between our world and the world of magic. Use your garden to communicate with the earth, harmonize your energy, and get in tune with the natural cycles of the earth.

# Houseplants

Though you can consider any plant you grow in a pot indoors a houseplant, this is also a name for a specific class of plant. Most varieties of houseplants have the ability to absorb pollutants from their environment, purifying the air we breathe. Studies have also shown that people are happier when there are plants in their living spaces. Though many of these plants have distinct magical uses, most of the benefits of these plants are emotional and energetic. Many houseplants require very specific containers, humidity levels, fertilizers, and hours of sunlight in a day and do not yield any sort of harvest you can use in your spells and rituals. What you get instead is cleaner air and an ever-growing source of positive energy.

Tropical palms bring strong solar energy into your home, breaking up stale energy and keeping your home safe from nasty spiritual entities. The African violet is associated with love and magic, and its vibrant purple flowers pull lunar energy into your home. Aloe, a succulent that grows in long spears, is associated with the moon and the element of water because the gel inside the leaves is cooling and healing. The clusters of star-shaped flowers that grow on the long tendrils of the hoya, also called a wax plant, produce truly intoxicating nectar with an aroma that fills the whole house and bestows blessings on anyone who smells it.

YULE

SAMHAIN

IMBOLC

December 21 | February 2

October 31 | March 21

MABON

OSTARA

September 21 | May 1

August 1 | June 21

LUGHNASADH

BELTANE

LITHA

## Chapter Three

# Connecting with the Natural World

A connection to the natural world is at the center of green witchcraft. This chapter explains how to create and cultivate a strong connection.

# Making Contact

Your connection to the natural world grants you access to the energy all around you for spiritual purposes, but it also helps you tap into the magic inside you. Studies show that connecting with nature helps decrease acute anxiety and depression while improving focus and memory. Sharing space with plants provides us with cleaner breathing air and more balanced humidity levels. This, combined with the positive psychological effects of proximity to plants, can help facilitate and speed up the healing process. Connecting with nature makes us happier, calmer, smarter, and stronger.

One of the reasons that going outside into nature or bringing nature into our space is so beneficial to our psychological health is that it encourages us to practice mindfulness. Being mindful is being focused entirely on the present moment; in other words, it's stopping to smell the roses, just for the joy of it. Much like meditation, mindfulness can help us tune in to the unseen energies of the world along with the natural beauty all around us. We're more likely to get to this state spontaneously when we're surrounded by natural life, but you can also consciously practice mindfulness with the help of houseplants. Take, for example, the traditional Japanese art of bonsai. Growers find that making time to tend to their miniature tree, and to use their intuition to decipher the true spirit of the plant, clears the mind of anxiety and teaches them patience and creativity.

# Exploring Your World

We talk a lot about earth-bound magic and energy in this book, but none of that would exist without the magic of the entire universe. To celebrate and align ourselves with the energy of the earth, we need to take time to realize the small part we play in this very BIG universe. This section covers a few of the ways in which witches can connect to these energies that often feel out of our grasp.

## Seasons, Solstices & Equinoxes

Marking the seasons, solstices, and equinoxes is one of my favorite places to start when it comes to practically aligning ourselves with the earth's energy. The Wiccan religion follows a calendar known as the Wheel of the Year, which features eight holy days, or Sabbats, that honor the seasons and their European ancestral traditions. The imagery and idea behind the Wheel of the Year have become widely accepted by witches from all walks of life as a way to connect to and celebrate the earth.

Four of the Sabbats are based on European fire festivals and legends from Celtic and Greek mythology: Imbolc to mark the start of spring on February 1 or 2, Beltane on May 1 to observe the start of the summer, Lughnasadh or Lammas on August 1 to mark the beginning of the harvest season, and Samhain or Halloween on October 31 to close out the harvest season. These holidays are spiritual and emotional in nature and usually involve celebrating our connection to the earth around a fire.

The other four Sabbats are based on solar events, known as solstices and equinoxes, and the changing of the seasons. They are Ostara, or the spring equinox, between March 19 and 22; Litha, or the summer solstice, between June 19 and 23; Mabon, or the autumn equinox, between September 19 and 23; and Yule, or the winter solstice, between December 20 and 23. These days are extra special to many who practice green witchcraft as they mark the life and movement of the earth within the universe. On the equinoxes, the day and night are of an equal length because Earth's equator lines up perfectly with those of the sun, and so these are the days on which we focus on balance. The solstices mark when the sun is at its highest peak over one of the poles. In the Northern Hemisphere, this happens on the summer solstice, and as a result, we have the longest day (and shortest night) of the year in June. During the winter solstice, the Southern Hemisphere has its longest day, while northerners are plunged into winter darkness. On these days, we focus on harmony, and there's always an element of celebrating our gratitude for the earth.

This is just one way to explore and experience the seasons without the need to give up or replace your favorite holidays. You can add these to your calendar or inject some of the meaning and symbolism into the holidays you already celebrate, like Christmas (Yule), Easter (Ostara), and Thanksgiving (Mabon).

## The Sun, Moon & Stars

Thinking about what lies beyond our atmosphere and the vastness of space can be scary and dizzying. However, knowing how small we truly are also reminds us that we're a part of something bigger. While very few may have the opportunity to experience the cosmos firsthand, astronomy and astrology allow you to connect with the universe from wherever you happen to be.

Astronomy is the scientific field of study concerning space and the stars. This is the study of the physical planets, stars, asteroids, and everything else that shares our universe. Start by watching the movement and actions of the sun and moon by paying attention to solar events like eclipses and the changing moon phases. Make time to observe the stars and constellations and cosmic events like meteor showers. Get a telescope so you can get a closer look or visit a planetarium if your town has one.

Astrology is not a scientific field, though up until about 150 years ago, it was considered to be one of the oldest sciences in the world. Every civilization that we know of has looked to the stars for meaning and guidance. This is an intuitive field of study concerning the movements and positions of celestial bodies and their influence on human lives and emotions. Your horoscope, based on the tropical zodiac, is only a small part of personal astrology, but it's the best place to start. Learn your sun sign, or main zodiac sign, and start to follow astrological advice on a regular basis. (I like to check mine daily, weekly, and monthly.) This is a large field of study, but the following list can help you get started with some basics about the sun signs.

## In the Wild

Everyone has different ideas as to what counts as "wilderness." Whether you're into deep-woods camping or glamping in the backyard, you can always acquaint yourself with the wild energy of the planet. This is where the knowledge you've amassed about your natural environment comes into play. You can also do small things like put out bird feeders at home or have plants in your garden that attract birds, animals, or pollinators to feel at one with the wild.

You must remember when it comes to connecting intimately with wilderness is that you are no longer in the domain of man. To stay safe in the wild, take inspiration from the animal kingdom and use all of your senses, along with your intuition, to guide you. Remain humble and curious, and you'll be a wild witch in no time.

# The Twelve Signs of the Zodiac

| Sun Sign | Birthday | Planet/Element |
| --- | --- | --- |
| ARIES | MAR 21–APR 19 | MARS/FIRE |
| TAURUS | APR 20–MAY 20 | VENUS/EARTH |
| GEMINI | MAY 21–JUN 20 | MERCURY/AIR |
| CANCER | JUN 21–JUL 22 | MOON/WATER |
| LEO | JUL 23–AUG 22 | SUN/FIRE |
| VIRGO | AUG 23–SEPT 22 | MERCURY/EARTH |
| LIBRA | SEPT 23–OCT 22 | VENUS/AIR |
| SCORPIO | OCT 23–NOV 21 | PLUTO/WATER |
| SAGITTARIUS | NOV 22–DEC 22 | JUPITER/FIRE |
| CAPRICORN | DEC 23–JAN 19 | SATURN/EARTH |
| AQUARIUS | JAN 20–FEB 18 | URANUS/AIR |
| PISCES | FEB 19–MAR 20 | NEPTUNE/WATER |

# Celtic Tree Zodiac

The Celtic tree zodiac is not as ancient of a practice as the Western zodiac but is a 20th-century invention. It's based on an ancient Celtic alphabet known as Ogham and the practice of worshipping sacred trees. This zodiac assigns these trees to a month of the year. An interesting date on this calendar is December 23, the day of the winter solstice, known as the nameless day, and associated with the highly toxic mistletoe. This is a day between the last day of the year and the first, and anything is considered possible.

# Celtic Tree Zodiac

| Tree | Birthday |
| --- | --- |
| BIRCH | DECEMBER 24–JANUARY 20 |
| ROWAN | JANUARY 21–FEBRUARY 17 |
| ASH | FEBRUARY 18–MARCH 17 |
| ALDER | MARCH 18–APRIL 14 |
| WILLOW | APRIL 15–MAY 12 |
| HAWTHORN | MAY 13–JUNE 9 |
| OAK | JUNE 10–JULY 7 |
| HOLLY | JULY 8–AUGUST 4 |
| HAZEL | AUGUST 5–SEPTEMBER 1 |
| VINE | SEPTEMBER 2–29 |
| IVY | SEPTEMBER 30–OCTOBER 27 |
| REED | OCTOBER 28–NOVEMBER 24 |
| ELDER | NOVEMBER 25–DECEMBER 22 |
| MISTLETOE | DECEMBER 23 |

## Characteristics

NEW BEGINNINGS, CREATIVITY, RENEWAL

INTELLECT, WISDOM, INFLUENCE, PROTECTION

ENCHANTMENT, MAGIC

HEALING, CREATIVITY, BALANCE, FAERIES

LOVE, HEALING, DIVINATION

FERTILITY, CREATIVITY, NEW LIFE, LOVE

WISDOM, LEADERSHIP, DIVINE POWER

PROTECTION, PATIENCE, ENDURANCE

INSPIRATION, CREATIVITY, PROSPERITY

GROWTH, EXPANSION, ETERNITY

SPIRITUAL EVOLUTION, EMPATHY, PSYCHIC ABILITY

ANCESTORS, CLEARING, BANISHING NEGATIVITY

HEALING, FAERIES, PROTECTION

THE WINTER SOLSTICE, NAMELESS DAY,
ANYTHING IS POSSIBLE

## By Land & By Sea

Life on land is a very solar experience, while life under the sea takes its cues from the moon. The moon is associated with the element of water, which is assigned the lunar qualities of depth, intuitive communication, and beauty in darkness. This isn't just a magical association. The gravitational pull of the moon affects the flow of water all over the planet with the tidal force. The tides are the rise and fall of water levels caused by the combined effects of the gravitational force of the moon and the rotation of the earth. The highest tides in the world travel through the Bay of Fundy, between New Brunswick and Nova Scotia on Canada's east coast. Every day, more than two billion tons of water flow in and out of the bay, creating a difference of 16 meters, or more than 50 feet. Not only does the water level rise this much, but it also falls this much, exposing part of the ocean floor.

Connecting with aquatic wilderness can be more challenging depending on your location, which is why so many people travel to locations known for scuba diving and visit commercial aquariums to explore the depths and connect with the creatures that live there.

# Finding Your Ground

Grounding is one of the most important ways for green witches to both receive and release magical energy. Grounding is a meditative practice where you create a connection with the planet using a combination of physical contact and visualization or imagination. This creates an invisible thread that allows you to bring energy up to you from the earth and release it back into the earth afterward. Think of it like a lightning rod, helping us channel the power of electricity and neutralize it when it becomes too much to handle safely.

I find grounding to be helpful both before and after any magical exercise and whenever I feel like I need to establish a stable foundation for myself. In moments of anxiety or chaos, grounding allows us to release that overwhelming energy into the earth. Once you figure out the best way to ground yourself, you'll know when you need it.

My favorite way to ground is by connecting to each of the elements. I do this by focusing on how each one feels, smells, or sounds. Let's try it right now.

1. Start by making yourself comfortable, with your feet planted flat on the ground, if possible. (Doing this outside would be ideal, of course, but it can be done anywhere because you're never really as far away from the elements as you might think.) Close your eyes, relax your shoulders, unclench your jaw, and let your hands fall at your sides. Let your back and legs settle and get comfortable.

2. Breathe slowly in through your nose and out through your mouth. Focus on the feeling of the air coming through your nose, filling your lungs and belly. Push the air out, and feel it blow past your teeth and tongue. Do this four times.

3. Keep breathing, but turn your attention to the heat of fire. Feel the heat of the sun shining above you or through the window, or the heat radiating from your own living body. Recall a memory of a time you sat in front of a roaring fire and could feel the heat on your face and legs. Breathe in and out four times slowly, allowing your whole body to feel the warmth.

4. Cool down with the refreshing energy of water. Recall how it feels to take that first step into the ocean or lake on a calm

day. Feel the cool water gently lapping at your ankles and then at your knees and lower back. Remember the sensation of standing beneath a waterfall or splashing saltwater on your face—refreshing and relaxing at the same time. Take four deep breaths and smell the salt or seaweed.

5. Take stock of your surroundings. Are you on a breezy beach with a bonfire going and sand between your toes? Or maybe you just stepped out of a luxurious bath, surrounded by flickering candles. Feel the solid ground beneath your feet, fully supporting you in this moment and in all the moments to come. Listen for the hum of the earth below and around you, and know that you're safe, supported, and connected to the planet. Breathe in through your nose and smell fresh-cut grass. Breathe out, sharing that breath with the trees that will use it to make oxygen. Take three more deep breaths, and when you're ready, open your eyes and come back to the present moment.

# Inviting the Energy

If you want to invite the elements into your space for spell work, grounding is a great place to start, but you can also bring in tactile representations of each of the elements.

The element of earth can be represented with a small bowl of dirt, sand, or salt, or the presence of any plants and stones. In the tarot, the earth suit is represented with plates or discs made from ceramic, clay, or cast metal. Food is also a powerful earth symbol. All of these symbols can be combined as you choose.

The element of air can be called in using wafting incense, a hand fan, bells, wind chimes, and naturally dropped feathers. Swords are the air suit in the tarot, and the knife or scissors from your toolkit have this same energy.

Fire as an element is usually represented with candles, but you can also include things like chile peppers, volcanic rocks or sand, or images of dragons. Wands are the fire suit in the tarot, so if you use a wooden wand, this can be your fire symbol, although you can also use the ace of wands tarot card.

Put a glass of fresh, clean water on your altar for this final physical element. Cups are the elemental symbol of water from the tarot, and some witches have a cup or chalice specifically for magical water. Collect seashells, driftwood, or seaweed, or use images of beaches and sea creatures. Mermaids, and their magical mirrors, symbolize water and are especially potent in beauty and love magic.

# Experiencing the Energy

During their practice, every green witch has asked the same question: "What does energy feel like?" I wish there were a concrete answer, but the truth is that it feels different for everybody. Our psychic senses are just like our physical senses and are influenced by our personality and natural environment as well as the energy of those around us. These three exercises focus on experiencing the colorful energy field, or aura, of another person. Don't look up any of the meanings about aura colors just yet to keep the experiment unbiased, but go to your local hardware store and get identical paint swatches in the main rainbow of colors and grab a friend who would like to know more about their aura.

* **Start with observation.** Without talking, show your friend each color and watch their reaction. Do they smile or frown? Hand them the color swatches and ask them to go through each one and silently recall a memory connected to each color.

Which colors do they linger on the longest? Finally, hold each color up to your friend one by one, and take stock of what you see. Is this a color they wear all the time or maybe one you know they really hate? Take note of which colors produce positive reactions in your friend and in you.

- **Sit close and put your hand on their shoulder (if they're comfortable allowing you to do so) to interact with your friend's energy.** Show them each color one at a time, but this time talk about their feelings and reactions. What does red make them think of? What memory is tied to the color green? Feel free to laugh or cry and discuss each color in as much depth as you want. Let yourself feel their laughter or their pain. Notice if their skin gets warm or cold, if they tense up, and what kind of movements they make during each conversation.

- **Think about all the colors and your friend's reactions, and choose a few that produced a positive reaction and that feel right to you.** Narrow it down to one and hold that color in your mind. Focus hard on it, and ask your friend what color they associate most with their identity. Whether you agree or each pick a different one, now's the time to look up the meanings of those aura colors. How did you do? What did you feel? What does your friend's energy feel like to you?

The energy around us is constantly changing based on our moods, beliefs, health, and spiritual development, and that includes our aura. At different points in your life, your aura may change color or size. For example, when you open up the psychic senses, purple will often appear in your aura around the crown chakra.

# Developing the Senses

A big part of green witchcraft is taking note of the ways in which the magical and material interact and even mirror each other. In this case, it's our senses, both the kind we use every day to navigate the world and the psychic kind. Our physiological senses are sight, smell, taste, touch, and sound. For every sense, there is a part of our body that takes in data and sends it to the brain, where it's analyzed so the information can be put to use. Since everyone's brain is unique, so, too, is everyone's perception of the world through these senses. Psychic senses are no different.

There are more than five psychic senses, and they're referred to as "the clairs," a term that comes from the French word for "clear."

- **Clairvoyance, or "clear seeing," is psychic sight.** This is perception based on images, but those images either are not visible to others or are seen only in the mind. Many people with a strong clairvoyant sense can see things like spirits, auras, and even visions of the past and future. The third eye chakra, located in the middle of the forehead, processes clairvoyant messages.

- **Clairaudience is psychic hearing.** This could be an inner voice that's always present or even the inner voices of others. For some, songs, words, and sounds heard with the physical ears can trigger psychic hearing, which processes the information through the throat chakra.

- **Clairtangency, or psychometry, is the ability to take in psychic information through touch.** Witches who can touch an item and get psychic impressions of its history or ownership are processing their psychic impressions through the skin, specifically the hand chakras.

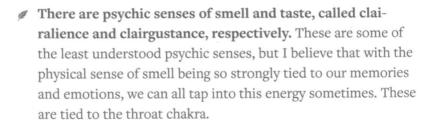

- There are psychic senses of smell and taste, called clairalience and clairgustance, respectively. These are some of the least understood psychic senses, but I believe that with the physical sense of smell being so strongly tied to our memories and emotions, we can all tap into this energy sometimes. These are tied to the throat chakra.

- Intuition (claircognizance) and psychic empathy (clairsentience) don't have corresponding physical senses because these are both emotional senses. Those with a strong intuition just know things. This sense originates with the solar plexus chakra and is the source of the good old-fashioned "gut feeling." To be an empath is to feel the emotions of the people around you as if they're yours. This ability is connected to the heart chakra, and it can be difficult to tell which feelings are theirs and which belong to someone else. These are the two most common psychic senses.

To help you identify and train your own psychic senses, try this simple method adapted from *The Natural Psychic* by Ellen Dugan (a book and author I recommend for green witches):

Grab a deck of tarot cards and find the moon. Choose two other cards at random, shut your eyes, and shuffle the three of them together. Lay them facedown in front of you and try to locate the moon. Look at the cards and see if anything stands out. Listen for an inner voice giving you direction. Pay attention to your solar plexus or stomach to see if you feel a pull toward one in particular. Reach your hands out and touch the backs of the cards and see if you receive a message that way. Pick one.

# Channeling the Sixth Sense

The sixth sense, also known as extrasensory perception or ESP, is a classic way of discussing the psychic senses. In the 1930s, two doctors of parapsychology at Duke University in North Carolina tried to prove the existence of ESP by getting a subject to correctly guess the symbols on a hidden card. Their tests proved unsuccessful, but the cards, called Zener cards after the designer, have been part of the image of psychic study ever since.

In 1999, a young Haley Joel Osment uttered the words "I see dead people" in the film *The Sixth Sense* and turned our attention to another psychic sense: mediumship. Mediums no doubt tend to possess other psychic senses, but what makes them unique is their ability to fully interact with the world of the dead. Many mediums can see and hear the spirits of the dead, both here on earth and in other planes of existence. They can sometimes help ghosts and lingering spirits move on to the afterlife and can also contact spirits who have crossed over to deliver messages for their loved ones.

# PART II

# Practicing Green Witchcraft

I n this part, we'll further explore the use of flowers, plants, herbs, and other natural elements in your green witchcraft practice for healing, spells, and more. I'll explain how to source specific materials as well as their energies and magical purposes. You'll also find safety tips, precautions, and best practices as well as practical exercises.

**W**hen selecting ingredients for your spells and rituals, the best way to know what will work for you is to study how something affects and is affected by the natural world and get in touch with your intuition. This is something witches call "magical correspondences." The same way a zodiac sign can give us a vague picture of who a person is, correspondences give us that for everything from plants and crystals to animals and actions. These are some common types of correspondences to incorporate into your practice.

**Botanical name:** This name is part of the scientific classification of all plants, and since common names can vary widely, this will help you know exactly which flower you're interacting with.

**Element:** Every flower is associated with at least one classical Western element: earth, air/wind, fire, water, and aether/spirit.

**Astrological:** Yes, flowers have zodiac signs, though they are not based on any birth date. Each one is associated with at least one of the tropical zodiac signs as well as planets.

**Chakra:** Every flower resonates with one or all of our chakra points and can be used for healing or balancing.

**Energies:** These are the talents or areas of expertise of a flower.

**Magical uses:** Every flower can be used in a variety of ways and at different stages of life. This section will tell you some of the ways witches use each flower.

## Chapter Four

# Flourishing with Flowers

In this chapter, I will introduce you to
15 different varieties of flowers, all with
their own energies and uses in magic.
Then you'll get a chance to connect
with the flowers on your own in acts of
magic, recipe making, and rituals.

# Flowers

Flowers, like witches, have their own distinct talents and personalities. Sometimes those personalities are even distinct from the plant they're attached to. That's why we'll discuss flowers separately. Even though some do grow on plants, herbs, or trees, the flowers themselves have a chemistry and magic all their own.

## Rose

**Botanical name:** *Rosa*

**Element:** water

**Astrological:** Venus; Libra, Taurus, Cancer

**Chakra:** all—crown, third eye, throat, heart, solar plexus, sacral, root, but especially heart

**Energies:** self-love, abundance, beauty, chakra balancing, blessing, dream magic, emotional and spiritual healing, healthy relationships, protection, purification, romantic love, spirituality

**Magical uses:** The rose is the queen of the flowers and an expert in all things related to love. Dried and fresh roses are used in a wide variety of spells and rituals, as are rose water and essential oil, because this flower is said to have the most positive energy of any living thing on the planet. It's incredibly aromatic and romantic.

## Jasmine

**Botanical name:** *Jasminum officinale*

**Element:** water

Astrological: Neptune, Moon; Pisces, Cancer

Chakra: crown, heart, sacral

Energies: abundance, sensuality, attraction, relaxation, sexual healing, divination, dream magic, luxury

Magical uses: Fresh jasmine really comes alive after dark, when it releases its intoxicating fragrance, which has led to it being called "Queen of the Night" and having lunar associations. The dried flowers can be used in incense blends, teas, and mojo bags, while jasmine essential oil is the star of the show in baths, perfumes, and potions. Many modern witches have come to see jasmine as a Neptunian, rather than lunar, flower because of its incredible powers of divination, psychic development, and dream magic.

## Lavender

Botanical name: *Lavandula angustifolia*

Element: air

Astrological: Mercury; Gemini, Virgo

Chakra: crown, third eye, throat, heart, solar plexus

Energies: sleep, divination, reducing anxiety, psychic awareness, happiness, purification, clarity, spiritual cleansing, magic, harmony, balance, healing, protection, reconciliation, moving on

Magical uses: I recommend lavender to every green witchcraft newcomer because of its wealth of uses and universal appeal. Lavender can be added to almost any magical working to provide stress relief, increase psychic abilities, clear out spiritual energy, and bring balance to a space. You can use lavender in the form of dried flowers, fresh stalks, and essential oils.

## Hoya

**Botanical name:** *Hoya carnosa*

**Element:** air

**Astrological:** Moon

**Chakra:** crown, solar plexus, root

**Energies:** chakra alignment, grounding, protection, moon magic, blessings, intuition, destiny, healing, star magic, reconciliation, setting boundaries

**Magical uses:** This popular houseplant grows long tendrils covered in dark green, waxy leaves and rounded clusters of tiny, white, star-shaped flowers. After dark, each flower hosts a single drop of nectar that fills the room with a clear and sweet scent. Hoya aligns all chakras and individually opens the crown chakra for magic, the solar plexus chakra for boundary setting, and the root chakra for grounding. The flowers are also known as pentagram flowers and are excellent for protection of the home and self.

## Hibiscus

**Botanical name:** *Hibiscus rosa-sinensis*

**Element:** water, fire

**Astrological:** Venus, Mars; Scorpio

**Chakra:** sacral

**Energies:** independence, freedom, personal glory, sensuality, harmony, passion, chakra balancing, magical catalyst, relaxation

**Magical uses:** The hibiscus is inviting, beautiful, and loving and also strong and confident. It's a perfect meeting of both the sensitive nature of water and the passionate force of fire. This flower can be added to potions and teas to balance the chakras and attract passionate love and sensual experiences, while also encouraging us to maintain our independence. As a magical catalyst, dried hibiscus flowers can be added to any spells and rituals for which you need quick results.

## Sunflower

**Botanical name:** *Helianthus annuus*

**Element:** fire

**Astrological:** Sun; Leo

**Chakra:** solar plexus

**Energies:** radiance, happiness, health, nourishment, strength, truth, summer solstice, fertility, abundance, protection, confidence, self-esteem

**Magical uses:** The sunflower has been grown by the indigenous peoples of Mexico and Peru for more than 4,000 years. The Aztecs grew sunflowers even before they grew corn, squash, and beans. When the Spanish came looking for gold, they found entire fields of it in this solar beauty. With thick stalks that can grow to be up to nine feet in height, sunflowers attract abundance, happiness, and good health when planted in the garden.

## Red Clover

**Botanical name:** *Trifolium pratense*

**Element:** air

**Astrological:** Mercury; Taurus

**Chakra:** throat

**Energies:** natural beauty, faeries, grounding, good luck, love and lust, healing a broken heart, health, protection, abundance, confidence

**Magical uses:** Red clover blossoms can be dried and used for tea, potions, baths, and incense blends. This flower has a very attractive quality and is good for bringing in blessings and love as well as pollinators, animals, and faeries. Clover has a long history as a medicine and can help speed magical and emotional healing. The leaves grow in groups of three and have always been a magical talisman, but four-leaf clovers are the ultimate symbol of magical luck.

## Datura **POISONOUS**

**Botanical name:** *Datura stramonium, D. innoxia, D. metel*

**Element:** water

**Astrological:** Venus, Saturn; Capricorn

**Chakra:** third eye

**Energies:** divination, enchantment, astral travel, personal power, wolf spirit, disguise, transformation, hex breaking, visions, dream magic

**Magical uses:** Datura, also known as jimsonweed, has been associated with witches and the ointments that make them (and their brooms) fly. Datura grows wild, and some types are considered a weed, but this flower can bring true ancient sorcery into your life. It is possible to handle Datura, but I recommend spending time near it, watching it, and listening for its messages without touching it at first, as the whole plant can be very toxic—even poisonous.

## Magnolia

**Botanical name:** *Magnolia grandiflora*

**Element:** earth

**Astrological:** Venus; Taurus

**Chakra:** heart, earth star

**Energies:** personal power, fidelity, ancient wisdom, past lives, strength, psychic healing, loving relationships

**Magical uses:** Magnolia is a truly ancient species. This beautiful, fragrant flower has thrived on earth longer than bees have existed and is still pollinated by beetles in the spring. The flowers and leaves can be used in all magic concerning love and happiness in relationships. When the flowers are in bloom, the scent of magnolia activates our own ancient wisdom and allows us to explore past lives.

## Borage

**Botanical name:** *Borago officinalis*

**Element:** air

**Astrological:** Jupiter, Sagittarius

**Chakra:** throat, third eye, heart

**Energies:** courage, star magic, energy, optimism, learning, domestic harmony, protection, heart healing, truthful self-expression, confidence, empathic healing and protection, eloquence

**Magical uses:** This beautiful blue starflower just makes people feel at ease. That's its greatest power, for when we feel at ease, we're better able to express ourselves, take in new information, summon courage, and heal from pain. The dried flower can be added to incenses and herbal blends and even carried as a talisman of protection—especially for those with empathic abilities. Fresh borage can be candied and eaten whenever you're studying magic to help you retain information.

## Echinacea

**Botanical name:** *Echinacea purpurea*

**Element:** fire

**Astrological:** Jupiter; Sagittarius

**Chakra:** throat

**Energies:** strength, amplification, clearing blockages, healing, support for healers, clairvoyance, psychic abilities, protection, courage, magical amplification and potency, love, abundance

**Magical uses:** Echinacea has a lot of powerful physical healing benefits, but it's also a flower of strong spiritual support. It can be added to teas, baths, and incense blends to help clear mental and emotional blockages holding you back, access insights and courage, and support on your healing journey. Add echinacea petals to any spell for amplification of the energy and to open psychic channels.

## African Violet

**Botanical name:** *Saintpaulia ionantha*

**Element:** water

**Astrological:** Moon, Venus; Capricorn

**Chakra:** crown

Energies: spirituality, love, beauty, psychic power, protection, higher learning, spring equinox, comfort

Magical uses: This delightfully fuzzy houseplant with bright purple flowers is talented at drawing positive spiritual energy into the home. Place an African violet on a windowsill on the night of the full moon to draw in lunar energy, and then add the fresh flowers to baths to invoke any of its energies.

## Calendula

Botanical name: *Calendula officinalis*

Element: fire

Astrological: Sun

Chakra: solar plexus, root

Energies: love divination, moving stagnant energy, spiritual protection, honoring and remembering the dead, Samhain and the Day of the Dead, happiness, heart healing, success, mediumship, dream magic, good luck

Magical uses: This is the signature flower of the Day of the Dead celebrations in Mexico on November 1 and 2. The bright colors and sweet smell of the calendula flower, or marigold, help spirits find their way to their families' altars and celebrations. The dried flower has medicinal properties and is a great addition to incense blends.

## Lotus

Botanical name: *Nelumbo nucifera*

Element: water

**Astrological:** Moon, Venus; Pisces

**Chakra:** crown

**Energies:** love magic, clarity, creativity, healing depression, purification, transformation, spiritual growth, guidance, divination, enlightenment

**Magical uses:** The lotus flower has been a sacred symbol of peace and spirituality in India since 1400 BC, and the Egyptians had their own sacred lotus (actually a water lily). Crown chakra is often depicted as a lotus to signal the height of spiritual enlightenment.

## Honeysuckle

**Botanical name:** *Lonicera periclymenum*

**Element:** water, earth

**Astrological:** Sagittarius; Venus

**Chakra:** sacral

**Energies:** activating intuition, sexual healing and awakening, prosperity, good luck, faeries, attracting love and sex, sweetening spells, attraction

**Magical uses:** The flowers of the honeysuckle vine produce sticky sweet nectar that's irresistible to animals and humans alike. It's a sweet, sexy flower that's best used when fresh in baths and sweetening spells. The scent is known to carry vivid dreams of love and lust in through windows on warm summer nights.

# Flowers in Practice

# Red Clover Glamour Potion

This potion combines red clover, pink salt, and fresh water to help you see and project your natural beauty, promote confidence and inner peace, attract love, and ground you in your body.

Glamour is much more than conventional outer beauty or expensive makeup and jewelry; it's the power of knowing how special you are and how to show that to the world. It's also a branch of magic all on its own that includes spells for beauty, bravery, confidence, eloquence, and charm. We're going to employ red clover and its connection to old-time faerie magic to help bring these qualities to the surface any time you need them.

This ritual is best done on a Friday—which is associated with Venus, water, and beauty—and with a clean face. Make sure to gently wash any dirt off the clover blossoms before you begin and to use fresh, clean water.

**You will need:**

- glass bowl
- 3 teaspoons pink Himalayan salt
- 1 cup filtered or spring water
- 3 fresh red clover blossoms, washed
- small pump spray bottle
- mirror
- clean cloth or paper towel
- rose water (optional)

1. Gather all your items in front of the mirror you use the most, take a deep breath, and look deeply and meaningfully at your reflection. Don't judge yourself. Avoid going through all the things you don't like about yourself. Simply take honest stock of your physical body. Now close your eyes and do the same for your nonphysical self—your feelings, thoughts, and intuition. How did looking at your reflection make you feel? Take your time.

2. Add the 3 teaspoons of pink salt to your glass bowl. Three is the number of creativity, change, and a connection to the natural forces of magic. Pour the water over the salt and stir it with your finger in a counterclockwise motion three times to activate the salt's cleansing energy.

3. Take all 3 clover blossoms into your hands and turn your attention back to your reflection. One at a time, place a clover blossom into the water and say something that you like about yourself—inside or out—or that makes you unique, beautiful, or glamorous. Stir the water with your finger again but in a clockwise motion, this time to activate clover's ability to attract good to you.

4. Splash a little of your potion onto the mirror with your fingers and then wipe it away, wiping away all your doubts and dislikes about yourself with it.

5. Put the rest of the potion, minus the clovers, into the spray bottle and lightly spritz your face and body. Look back at your reflection. Do you see anything different? Keep the potion in a cool, dry place for up to three weeks. Discard the clovers outside with other flowers.

Optional: If you'd like a bit of fragrance, rose water cools and hydrates your skin and hair and is a powerful ally in beauty rituals.

# Houseplant Home Protection

Hoya's pentagram-shaped flowers and fragrant honeydew nectar make it the perfect plant ally for setting boundaries around your home or space.

Witches use the pentagram, a five-pointed star, as a symbol of protection and a representation of the elements. Hoya's star-shaped flowers grow in round clusters that resemble the moon, so try to perform this spell after dark on the night of the full moon after spiritually cleansing your home.

**You will need:**

- potted hoya with open, nectar-producing flowers
- hand fan made of paper or fabric (not silk or satin)
- water that's been sitting on your altar or sanctuary

1. Find a flower cluster on your hoya in full bloom, with drops of nectar sitting on top of the flowers. Take time to admire the starry flowers, which really do seem to glow in the moonlight.

2. State your intention out loud: "You and I are going to fortify the boundaries of my home, keep me/my family safe, and allow only positive magical energy to enter here."

3. Press the open fan gently into the flowers, collecting the nectar on both sides.

4. Move clockwise through the home, drawing a pentacle in the air with the fan in front of every window and door. Feel free to invoke the elements out loud—earth, air, fire, water, and spirit—each time. You can also waft the scent toward yourself to protect your aura.

5. Return to your hoya when you're finished and give it some of your altar water as an offering of gratitude.

# Sacral Healing Bath Salts

This bath salt blend is formulated to balance and heal the sacral chakra, also known as the sex or water chakra, which sits just below your navel.

**You will need:**

- glass bowl and spoon for mixing
- 2 cups Himalayan salt
- 3 teaspoons olive or other carrier oil
- dried hibiscus flowers
- 3 drops jasmine essential oil
- 3 drops sandalwood essential oil
- 3 drops rose or rose geranium essential oil or 1 teaspoon rose water
- mason jar for storage
- hibiscus essential oil, Epsom salts, a small cotton bag, and dried heather flowers (optional)

1. Place 2 cups of Himalayan salt in pink or orange tones in your glass bowl. You can substitute Epsom salts, which help with physical relaxation, for some of the salt. Add the olive oil, 1 teaspoon at a time, and mix it with the salt. Don't let the oil pool at the bottom of the bowl or completely soak the salt; just cover it lightly.

2. Add a handful of hibiscus flowers—as much or as little as you like—and combine with the salt-and-oil mixture. This will turn your bath water a slight pink color. Add more if you would like a little extra color.

3. Add 3 drops each of jasmine and sandalwood oils. These are both very fragrant and associated with the energy of the moon (also aligned with this chakra), sensuality, and healing. Also add 3 drops of rose oil. Rose essential oil is notoriously expensive, so you can substitute rose geranium essential oil, which has a similar smell and energy, or a teaspoon of rose water. Rose balances all of the chakras and facilitates emotional healing.

4. Mix the salt blend well and transfer it to the jar. Leave the lid off for a day to let the salts dry a bit. Add a quarter cup of salts to your bath water, and make sure the water covers your navel. If you don't like having dried flowers floating in your bath water, put your salts in a cotton bag and hang it over the faucet as your tub is filling up. As you lie in the water, imagine a beautiful orange hibiscus slowly unfurling its petals in the area of your sacral chakra.

Optional: You can include hibiscus oil, though it has little fragrance and may not be very noticeable. Heather flower is considered a powerful healer for those who've experienced sexual harassment or assault.

# Rainbow Rose Ritual for Self-Love

This ritual brings the magic of roses into your bedroom to remind you that you don't need anyone else but yourself to shower you with love.

## You will need:

- 1 fresh rose in each color:

  - blue or lavender for enchantment

  - white for purification and new beginnings

  - pink for beauty and heart healing

- yellow for joy and friendship

- orange for energy and confidence

- red for unconditional love

- rainbow-dyed roses and a large mason jar (optional)

1. In the language of flowers, each color of the rose has a specific meaning, as does the size of the bouquet. Six roses represent the need we all have to be loved and cherished.

2. Make your bed up exactly the way you like it, bring the roses into your room, and close the door.

3. Grab your blue or purple rose, and detach the petals from the stem. Set the stem aside, sprinkle the petals over your bed, and say, "I am enchanting."

4. Continue down the list, saving red for last.

   - White: "This is a new beginning for me."

   - Pink: "I am beautiful, and my heart is open."

   - Yellow: "I am my own best friend and a great friend to others."

   - Orange: "I am constantly energized by the love I have for myself."

   - Red: "I love myself, even when others don't. I love myself unconditionally."

5. Lie down on your bed of roses and revel in their beauty. Take this time to love yourself.

   **Optional:** Rainbow-dyed roses can also be used and can carry special meaning for those on the LGBTQIA+ spectrum. You can dry the petals and display them in a mason jar to keep the spell going.

# Divination Dream Pillow

Divining the future or things unseen by magical means like crystal balls and tarot cards is called divination. Your dreams are naturally a powerful form of divination, and this ritual can help you recall and understand more of them.

Dream pillows are a type of magic that can heighten your dream-state intuition, encourage you to dream of certain things or events, and make sure you're able to recall more of your dreams the next day. I recommend getting a dream journal or making a section in your grimoire to keep track of the messages you receive.

**You will need:**

- a small, purple drawstring bag or purple fabric
- thread and needle (optional)
- dream journal and pen
- cotton balls or batting
- dried chamomile, lavender, and jasmine flowers
- jasmine, chamomile, and lavender essential oils
- tea ball, cup, and candles (optional)

1. Set aside a Monday night to create your divination pillow, as Mondays are associated with the moon and dreams.

2. Gather your tools on your altar space and light some candles to create a cozy and comfortable atmosphere, if you like. If you're sewing your pillow, start by sewing up three of the sides to make a little bag.

3. Open your journal or grimoire to a fresh page, and write down anything you might want to dream about or a problem on which you'd like some clarity. You might want to ask about a relationship or job.

4. Start filling your pillow with the cotton when you're ready but stop when it's half full.

5. Grab a pinch of each of the three herbs—chamomile for peaceful sleep and protection from nightmares, lavender for relaxation and opening the third eye, and jasmine for its connection to the dreamy magic of Neptune—and add them to the pillow. These flowers aren't just good for dream magic; each has a fragrance that helps you fall asleep and feel relaxed.

6. Add 2 drops of each essential oil to a piece of cotton and add that to the bag as well.

7. Tear the page from your journal with your dream intentions on it, fold it small, and add it to the pillow before filling it the rest of the way with cotton and closing up the end.

8. Place your dream pillow underneath your physical pillow and let the scents and energies of the flowers lull you into psychic dreams.

   Optional: These three flowers can all be brewed into an herbal tea, and together they make the perfect cup of sleepy-time comfort. Add equal parts of each flower to a tea ball and steep the flower mixture in hot water for two minutes. Drink it before bed to help engage all the senses in your dream magic.

## Chapter Five
# The Power of Plants

Witches have been harnessing the power
of plants for magic and medicine since
ancient times. With their roots firmly
planted in the earth and their leaves reaching
up to the heavens, plants connect us to
both the physical and spiritual worlds.

# Plants

Though flowers are indeed plants in a broader sense, the following 15 are larger and heartier, and more of the plant, such as stems and roots, is used in witchcraft.

## Mugwort

**Botanical name:** *Artemisia vulgaris*

**Element:** fire, earth

**Astrological:** Moon; Capricorn

**Chakra:** third eye

**Energies:** psychic power, dream magic, healing, astral projection, summer solstice, visions, healing, safe travel, women's health, birth, protection, cleansing magical tools

**Magical uses:** To me, there is no "witchier" magical herb than mugwort. It can be brewed into a tea or added to smoking blends to increase psychic awareness, bring on prophetic dreams, and help you recall them. Mugwort is a talisman for safe travel, both in your waking life and in dreams. Mugwort has long been used in traditional Chinese medicine to increase the flow of qi (vital life force) to certain parts of the body to facilitate healing through the process of moxibustion, which entails heating plant material near or on the skin's surface.

## Sage

**Botanical name:** *Salvia officinalis, S. apiana*

**Element:** air, earth

Astrological: Jupiter; Sagittarius

Chakra: crown

Energies: wisdom, cleansing, home blessing, longevity, protection, good luck, ancestral magic, banishing spirits, purification, grounding, mental clarity

Magical uses: All varieties of sage represent the wisdom of elder and ancient generations. When dried, sage is burned to clear the spiritual residue from an area, cleanse the aura, and offer spiritual protection. It opens us up to receiving spiritual messages while remaining firmly grounded. One of its most frequent uses is to clear lingering spirits and entities from a new home before moving in.

## Coffee

Botanical name: *Coffea arabica, C. canephora*

Element: fire, earth, air

Astrological: Uranus, Mercury; Sagittarius, Aquarius

Chakra: root, sacral

Energies: removing blockages, divination, grounding, mental clarity, prosperity, protection against nightmares, energizing spells, speeding and shaking things up, breaking curses

Magical uses: Your morning coffee is already a magical potion that energizes you and brings mental clarity. Adding whole coffee beans or even brewed coffee can help speed up any spells you're casting while helping you clarify your intention. If you don't enjoy drinking coffee, the plant can be grown inside and the leaves and flowers can be used for the same effects.

## Damiana

**Botanical name:** *Turnera diffusa*

**Element:** fire, water

**Astrological:** Venus, Jupiter; Scorpio

**Chakra:** sacral

**Energies:** meditation, divination, attracting love and sex, lucid dreaming, healing relationships, relaxation, Beltane

**Magical uses:** Damiana is one of my favorite plants for all kinds of love magic, like baths, herbal blends, and mojo bags. It's got a very sexy and mystical quality to it, probably because even the dried leaf smells like fresh figs. It can be made into tea or added to smoking blends, though it does have a slight physical relaxation effect when smoked.

## Mullein

**Botanical name:** *Verbascum thapsus*

**Element:** fire

**Astrological:** Saturn, Pluto; Capricorn

**Chakra:** third eye

**Energies:** protection, spirit communication, divination, spiritual cleansing, mediumship, dream magic, psychic connection

**Magical uses:** Fluffy dried mullein leaves make an excellent base for incense blends, as they have very little aroma but carry a whole lot of magical energy. Mullein is a very psychic nighttime herb used in mediumship and to clear spirits from haunted houses. The tall stalks can be dried, dipped in beeswax, and used as torches.

# Hemp

Botanical name: *Cannabis sativa*

Element: earth, water

Astrological: Saturn, Venus; Capricorn, Gemini

Chakra: all but especially the crown

Energies: magical amplification, manifestation, healing, money and abundance, clearing negative energy, love and sex, protection, sleep, death and saying goodbye, communication with spirits, meditation

Magical uses: Hemp, along with its psychoactive cousin usually referred to as cannabis, is among the oldest industrial and spiritual crops in the world. Hemp seeds are still being found in ancient dig sites, and it seems that it was an important plant in funeral practices for saying goodbye and honoring the dead. Hemp and cannabis* (where legal) can be used in your practice as the herbal equivalent of a quartz crystal because their uses are endless and they can take on any magical property you need. Growing hemp around the home attracts money and abundance, clears negative energy, and encourages restful sleep and speedy healing. You need not ingest any intoxicants to work with its energy if that's not right for you, as hemp on its own can be used dried in incense and herbal blends and as magical rope or twine. Additionally, hemp seed hearts are tasty and nutritionally dense and can be added to almost any food. The psychoactive cannabis has been used in meditation, love and sex magic, and communication with spirits since ancient times, and is currently used as a powerful and multipurpose medicine.

*Psychoactive *Cannabis sativa* may be illegal where you live, so always check your local laws and regulations.

## Rose of Jericho

**Botanical name:** *Selaginella lepidophylla*

**Element:** water, air

**Astrological:** Pluto; Scorpio

**Chakra:** root

**Energies:** abundance, resurrection and rebirth, blessings, success, strength, transformation, attraction, love and sex, money, healing, protection

**Magical uses:** This isn't a rose at all but rather a fern from the Chihuahua desert of Mexico called "the resurrection plant." When dry, the rose of Jericho looks like a small tumbleweed and appears to be dead, but once you place the roots in water, the plant comes alive, turning green and opening up. The resurrection plant attracts good fortune, love, and blessings to anyone who tends it.

## Tea Plant

**Botanical name:** *Camellia sinensis*

**Element:** fire, water

**Astrological:** Mars, Moon; Libra

**Chakra:** heart, solar plexus

**Energies:** healing, relaxation, energizing, memory and mental clarity, courage, money, prosperity, love, cleansing, aura healing, connection with spirits, psychic abilities

**Magical uses:** Most varieties of tea—black, green, white, and oolong—are made from the leaves of the *Camellia sinensis*. Other *Camellia* varieties produce ornate flowers popular in bouquets and in magic, and their healing heart chakra associations extend to the tea varieties. In addition to potions and beverages, tea can be added to baths, incenses, and herbal blends.

## Bladderwrack

Botanical name: *Fucus vesiculosus*

Element: water, air

Astrological: Moon; Pisces

Chakra: sacral

Energies: sea magic, health, wind, travel, psychic power, protection, money and prosperity, psychic healing, making wishes

Magical uses: This common seaweed is a great representation of the water element on your altar and doubles as a powerful talisman for a wide variety of magical uses. As a great source of iodine, it has many medicinal uses, and this energy carries over to its magical talents as well.

## Rue

Botanical name: *Ruta graveolens*

Element: fire

Astrological: Mars, Saturn; Aries

Chakra: root, third eye

Energies: protection, boundaries, visions, hex breaking, removing spiritual entities, psychic power

Magical uses: In Italian folk magic, rue is the ultimate protection against the evil eye, a type of curse. Its protection powers span the spiritual, physical, and emotional realms. Rue can be grown in the garden for this purpose, but you can also hang a dried sprig above doors and use the dried plant in incenses and powders for protection. The living plant produces a sap that can irritate the skin, so both people and animals tend to avoid it.

## Eye of Newt/Black Mustard

Botanical name: *Brassica nigra*

Element: fire

Astrological: Mars, Pluto; Aries

Chakra: root, third eye

Energies: witchcraft, psychic power, protection, magical camouflage, the new or black moon, Samhain, keeping secrets

Magical uses: The ultimate ingredient in a witch's brew, black mustard seed was quaintly known as eye of newt during the time of Shakespeare. This alone makes it appropriate to commence any acts of magic, but it is especially useful for calling upon psychic power and protection. A small amount of eye of newt can be added to incense blends, but it is pungent. Use it to cast a circle of protection around your home on the night of the new moon.

## Cinnamon

Botanical name: *Cinnamomum cassia*

Element: fire

Astrological: Sun, Mars; Aries

Chakra: heart, solar plexus, sacral

Energies: passion, creativity, money, good luck, sexuality, attraction, love, home protection, victory, speeding up, Mabon, Samhain

Magical uses: Fiery cinnamon is warm, passionate, energizing, and cozy. You can use the common powdered variety or the sticks, or even find large pieces of cinnamon bark for use in incenses and oil blends. A broom made of cinnamon protects the home and attracts prosperity.

## Witch Hazel

Botanical name: *Hamamelis virginiana*

Element: water

Astrological: Saturn; Capricorn

Chakra: heart

Energies: healing, beauty, divination, initiation, inspiration, cleaning, spiritual cleansing, heart healing, slowing down

Magical uses: Witch hazel is one of the most-used medicinal herbs in the world. Its main uses are in healing and soothing the skin, usually in a skin toner with alcohol and rose water. The twigs of this slow-growing shrub were once used for divining rods—magical tools for finding water—and the dried leaves go well in potions and waters.

## Broom Corn

Botanical name: *Sorghum bicolor*

Element: earth, air

Astrological: Cancer; Mercury

Chakra: root, crown

Energies: cleansing, astral travel, protection, hearth magic, love, weddings, harmony in the home, dream magic

Magical uses: Broom corn is, of course, used to make witch's brooms. This ornamental grass makes for perfect bristles on brooms for both magical and practical uses and has the ability to reach through the physical to the astral plane. During witchy weddings, it is customary to have couples jump over a specially decorated broom to signify entering into their new life and leaving behind the old.

## Orris/Queen Elizabeth Root

Botanical name: *Rhizoma iridis*

Element: water

Astrological: Moon; Venus

Chakra: heart

Energies: love drawing, psychic communication, women's empowerment, divination, psychic protection, passion, good luck, energy healing, wisdom, inspiration

Magical uses: Queen Elizabeth, or orris, root comes from the lovely blue iris, which is used for spiritual balance and cleansing. The root, on the other hand, is a powerful attraction talisman, especially for love and passion. The whole or powdered herb can be added to incenses, sachet powders, baths, and candle spells.

# Plants in Practice

## Sacred Smoke Cleansing Wand

You no doubt have seen bundles of sage burned to cleanse
the energy of a person or area with the smoke. These are
usually made with white sage, which is sacred to many Native
American tribes, and used in what's called a "smudging" cere-
mony.* Burning sacred herbs, however, has been a common
practice all over the world for a very long time. This sacred
plant bundle includes sage for cleansing, mugwort for protection and strengthening intuition, and lavender for happiness
and harmony, all tied into a wand shape. These plants are
powerful healers.

**You will need:**

- fresh mugwort, sage, and
  lavender stalks

- string (purple, if you
  have it)

- scissors

- fireproof bowl and matches

1. Harvest or buy fresh mugwort and sage of whatever variety is most common where you live, along with lavender stalks about 6 inches in length.

2. Gather your plants with the stalks pointing toward you in whatever order you feel called to. (Remember that this has to dry completely, so be mindful of how dense you make your bundle.)

3. Use your string to tie off the "handle" of your wand about an inch from the bottom, and then loosely wrap it around to the top and back down. Tie it off and cut off any excess string.

4. Let your wand dry for 4 to 8 weeks.

5. When it's completely dry, light your cleansing wand at the tip over a fireproof dish. Waft the smoke around your home to cleanse it of negative energy and add the healing energy of these sacred plants to your space.

*See Sage (page 78) for more on different sage varieties.

# Cimaruta Charm Bag

The Cimaruta (Chee-mah-roo-tah) is an Italian folk charm that's worn as jewelry or hung in the home to offer protection against the evil eye. This charm bag includes dried rue and protective talismans.

Given that its namesake, Saturn, is the planet of boundaries, this protection charm is best made on a Saturday night in your own kitchen, which is a place of power in Italian folk magic.

**You will need:**

- flannel bag in red, black, or cobalt blue
- dried rue, rosemary, and vervain
- charms or beads shaped like a crescent moon, hand, and eye
- hemp twine
- an antique key

1. Start by adding a couple of pinches of rue to your bag and breathe in the smell. Add a pinch of rosemary to keep away negative energy and enlist the aid of helpful ancestors. A pinch of vervain heightens the element of protection, especially in matters concerning the end of a relationship.

2. Add your charms. You can use anything that feels protective to you. These are just a few standard symbols from classic Cimaruta charms.

   - A crescent moon as a symbol of divine guidance and intuition

   - A hand to stop any curses or people who wish to do harm in their tracks

   - The nazar, a Turkish symbol to protect against the evil eye made of cobalt blue glass. Any eye imagery is a symbol against curses or ill will, as you're always under a watchful eye.

3. Activate the charm by lightly spitting (or mimicking spitting) three times into the bag. Imagine the rue coming to life and wrapping its protective branches around the charms inside. Wrap the hemp twine around the end three times and attach your antique key to make sure your protection spell doesn't keep good doors from opening to you.

# Hemp Rope Knotwork Spell

This spell uses the manifestation and meditation properties of hemp to cast a spell with your intention. It uses imagery of the tarot, making it totally customizable.

**You will need:**

- tarot deck

- hemp twine

- scissors

- plants, flowers, herbs, small crystals, feathers, a lock of hair, charms that match your intention, candle or wax seal, crystal beads (optional)

1. Choose a tarot card that represents you. This could be because of the image on the card or the meaning behind it. You may also choose one at random.

2. Set your intention and pick a corresponding card. The lovers or two of cups are good for love spells, the ace of pentacles for a new job, the chariot for travel, or the world for achievement. You can also choose a card you wish to be like, such as the empress or emperor.

3. Select a length of twine intuitively, or choose a number that means something to your spell, like the numbers on the cards, your birth month, or the date of your job interview. Tie knots in groups of three at equal intervals, stating your intention out loud and locking it into the twine as you go.

4. Repeat the previous step until you reach the end of the twine and then wrap it around your cards and tie it three final times, repeating your intention each time.

5. Carry this talisman with you or place it on your altar until your spell comes true. Don't untie your knots unless you want the spell, or relationship you've built, to come undone. Instead, slip the spell off your cards and bury it in the ground.

   Optional: You can use beads made of appropriate crystals and put them between the knots and keep the spell as a bracelet or charm afterward. You can also use each knot to tie magical items to your spell, such as leaves, feathers, small crystals, or charms.

# Resurrection Plant Growth Spell

This seven-day spell encourages growth in love or prosperity with the resurrection plant and green-growing agate.

Though the rose of Jericho looks like tumbleweed now, over the next seven days, you will water and tend it and watch it grow as if by magic, along with your money, love life, or career opportunities.

**You will need:**

- piece of paper and pen
- shallow, clear glass bowl
- pieces of tumbled tree and/or moss agate
- filtered water
- rose water
- dried rose of Jericho
- photos, business card, and dollar bill (optional)

1. Gather your items in a room appropriate for your intentions, like the bedroom for love, the bathroom for beauty, and the office for money or careers. Begin with the grounding exercise, and try to imagine the rose of Jericho opening wide as your connection to earth deepens.

2. Write whatever it is you'd like to see grow on a small square piece of paper, and sign your name. If you're trying to make the relationship with a specific person or employer flourish, you can add their name as well. Place the paper under the bowl with your words facing up. You may also add a business card for your new business venture or the company you hope hires you or a photo of someone with whom you're trying to grow.

3. Place a single stone in your bowl or cover the bottom with them. Moss agate is the stone of growth, especially in financial or career matters, and is a natural water filter. Tree agate is the stone of growing relationships and families and for bringing people in from far away.

4. Pour a shallow layer of water into the bowl and add a splash of rose water for blessings and positive energy. Then place the rose of Jericho in the bowl so the roots are just covered with water. Every day for seven days, switch out the water for new filtered water and use the old water to feed your other plants or to make a wash or spray for your home or business. After the seventh day, let your rose of Jericho dry up and rest for three days. Repeat this spell as often as you need to.

# Gardening by the Moon

The moon's tidal force affects all the water on the earth, and that includes the water in the soil and air. These charts can help you harness the energy of the moon for healthier plants and bigger harvests.

| Moon Phase | Gardening Tips |
|---|---|
| New Moon | At the new moon, the tidal force pulls water up and into seeds, and the increasing moonlight helps balance the growth of the roots and plant. |
| Waxing Crescent | The extra moisture in the ground makes the time between the new and full moon a great time for planting aboveground-bearing fruit plant seeds like strawberries as well as annual flowers. |
| Full Moon | The tidal force is high again, but the decreasing moonlight puts more focus on the roots. Plant bulbs and biennial and perennial flowers. This is also a favorable time for transplanting. |
| Waning Crescent | As you approach the new moon again, take time to prune, harvest, and fertilize your soil. This is also a good time to rest before the cycle starts again. |

The moon also moves between astrological phases every two and a half days, and this can be another factor in the moon's effects on your garden. (The moon sign for every day can be found in the Farmers' Almanac, or using online astrological calendars—I recommend Lunarium.)

| Astrological Element | Gardening Tips |
|---|---|
| Fire | These days are hot, dry, and barren. Use fire days for weeding, pest control, and canning your harvest. |
| Water | These days encourage extra growth and your water will go further. Water days are also great for pruning and transplanting to encourage growth. |
| Air | These are good days for weeding, tilling, and harvesting herbs for drying. |
| Earth | These are your most fruitful days, and are perfect for planting trees, bushes, and vines, as well as root and culinary crops. Virgo, however is barren, and provides time to rest. |

## Chapter Six

# Healing with Herbs & Greens

Herbs are small perennial and biennial plants that are usually full of fragrance and flavor. They can be blended into incenses and spells or used to add that energy to meals and beverages.

## Basil

**Botanical name:** *Ocimum basilicum*

**Element:** fire, water

**Astrological:** Mars; Aries, Scorpio

**Chakra:** heart

**Energies:** wealth, success, beauty, luck, love, protection, happiness, luck while traveling, reconciliation

**Magical uses:** Basil is one of the first herbs recommended to new witches because it's easy to grow, harvest, or buy and is very useful in practical magic. Its energy is generally positive and is good at attracting money and love. Keep a basil plant by the door to ensure that you always look your best when you leave the house.

## Rosemary

**Botanical name:** *Rosmarinus officinalis*

**Element:** air, fire

**Astrological:** Sun, Moon; Libra, Leo

**Chakra:** heart, third eye, solar plexus

**Energies:** remembrance, cleansing, strength, virtue, wisdom, protection, banishing, home, ancestors, cleansing magical tools, love

**Magical uses:** Rosemary is the jewel of the Mediterranean, and in Italy it's said that rosemary grows near homes filled with strong women. It's been associated with memory and remembrance; recall that Shakespeare declared, "Rosemary, that's for remembrance." It can be added to baths, mojo bags, and incense blends to honor and remember the dead as well.

## Alfalfa

**Botanical name:** *Medicago sativa*

**Element:** earth

**Astrological:** Venus, Jupiter; Taurus

**Chakra:** heart

**Energies:** rabbit magic, prosperity, good luck, grounding, protection from hunger and poverty, abundance, earth healing, growth, speed

**Magical uses:** Alfalfa is one of the world's oldest crops. Its name means "father of foods," as it feeds most livestock. It can be burned, carried, or added to washes and sprays to encourage money flow and to keep from going hungry.

## Five-Finger Grass

**Botanical name:** *Potentilla*

**Element:** air, water

**Astrological:** Venus, Uranus; Gemini

**Chakra:** heart, solar plexus

**Energies:** manifestation, good luck, money drawing, protection, uncrossing, Beltane, hex breaking, love, creativity, liberation, wildness, attraction, dreaming, divination

**Magical uses:** Also known as cinquefoil, five-finger grass is all about bringing in blessings, whether they deal with love, money, wisdom, protection, or just joy. You can use the dried plant as a talisman or in incense, and the oil can be added to hand and home washes, candles, and oil lamps to attract what you seek.

## Bay Laurel

Botanical name: *Laurus nobilis*

Element: fire

Astrological: Sun; Leo

Chakra: solar plexus, third eye

Energies: victory, money, confidence, wishes, protection, empowerment, divination, dream magic, success, empowerment for young boys, healing, spiritual cleansing

Magical uses: Bay leaves are powerful magical tools: Burned on their own or in incense blends and carried as talismans, they attract good fortune and blessings while protecting from the negative or scary. Write a wish on a bay leaf and burn it to ensure the wish comes true.

## Motherwort

Botanical name: *Leonurus cardiaca*

Element: water

Astrological: Venus; Leo

Chakra: heart, sacral

Energies: protection, women's empowerment, healing, nurturing, spiritual healing, astral travel, soothing anxiety, confidence, longevity

Magical uses: The "mom" of the magical plant world, its nurturing, healing, and empowering energy is great in baths, bags, and incenses. Use it in spells to heal physical and emotional illness and make those suffering feel less alone.

## Catnip

**Botanical name:** *Nepeta cataria*

**Element:** water

**Astrological:** Venus, Moon

**Chakra:** third eye, heart, sacral

**Energies:** charm, enchantment, cat magic, love, attraction, beauty, clarity, sleep, dream magic, divination

**Magical uses:** Catnip is all about the moon, night, and fantasy. It's great in teas, baths, incenses, and smoking blends to attract love, make you more charming to others, or put you in the right mindset for magic. Catnip can help harness the magic of cats and attract a familiar animal.

## Chamomile

**Botanical name:** *Matricaria chamomilla, Chamaemelum nobile*

**Element:** water

**Astrological:** Sun; Leo

**Chakra:** throat

**Energies:** money, sleep, good luck, love, purification, relaxation, protection, hex breaking, health, dream protection

**Magical uses:** Chamomile can be added to baths and incense blends to help you sleep peacefully and without disruptions from spiritual entities and nightmares. Its sunny disposition is perfect for attracting good luck and money, breaking up darkness, and physical and emotional healing.

## Lemongrass

**Botanical name:** *Cymbopogon nardus*

**Element:** air

**Astrological:** Mercury; Gemini

**Chakra:** throat

**Energies:** purification, psychic power, luck, protection, road opener, uncrossing, Mercury retrogrades, dream magic, lust, romance, cleansing, banishing

**Magical uses:** Lemongrass and its derivative, citronella, are the best at clearing up confusion, smoothing out chaotic energy, and opening roads and lines of communication. That's why it's a main ingredient in Van Van oil, one of the most commonly used dressing oils in hoodoo. Lemongrass can be added to oils, baths, and incense blends and is especially effective during Mercury retrogrades.

## Comfrey

**Botanical name:** *Symphytum officinale*

**Element:** water

**Astrological:** Saturn; Capricorn

**Chakra:** root

**Energies:** traveler protection, good luck, protection, grounding, money drawing, holding onto what you have, stability, endurance

**Magical uses:** Comfrey is a powerful physical healer in salves and poultices, and in magic, it provides protection and good luck. Use the dried leaves and roots in spells to bring in or keep money, sell a home, or get a job in a faraway location. A comfrey salve rubbed on the feet can help you feel grounded and find your way in unknown territory.

## Plantain

**Botanical name:** *Plantago*

**Element:** earth

**Astrological:** Venus, Mercury; Taurus

**Chakra:** sacral, throat

**Energies:** healing, strength, protection, fertility, invisibility, beauty, energy

**Magical uses:** Plantain is an incredibly prolific herb throughout the world that is generally considered a weed or pest. It grows in fields and parking lots and between the cracks of sidewalks. It's actually a very powerful herb for healing the skin from rashes, bites, and bruises and can be used to bring an extra kick of magical energy to any spell.

## St. John's Wort

**Botanical name:** *Hypericum perforatum*

**Element:** fire

**Astrological:** Sun; Leo

**Chakra:** solar plexus

**Energies:** healing, divination, happiness, the summer solstice, weather magic, protection

Magical uses: St. John's wort is another herb we've been using medicinally for centuries for everything from easing depression to soothing topical pain. In magic, it's one of the ultimate solar symbols and is included in bonfires and incenses for the summer solstice. It can be brewed into a tea or burned as incense.

## Mint

Botanical name: *Mentha*

Element: air

Astrological: Taurus

Chakra: throat, third eye

Energies: luck, money, healing, happiness, travel, energizing spells, prosperity, mental clarity, hex removal, communication, self-expression, clearing the way

Magical uses: Though each mint has its own properties, they all share connections to money and prosperity, travel, and communication. You can use mint fresh, dried, or in oil form in everything from baths to incenses to room sprays. Some mints have a strong menthol aroma, which is great for removing spiritual and emotional blockages that are keeping your intentions from coming to fruition.

## Vervain

Botanical name: *Verbena officinalis, Verbena hastata*

Element: water

**Astrological:** Venus; Gemini

**Chakra:** sacral, third eye

**Energies:** protection, purification, love, sleep, study, healing, lust, the summer solstice, inspiration, dream magic, passion, divination

**Magical uses:** Vervain provides protection, love, purification, and mental clarity. It can be brewed into a tea and added to baths or burned in incense blends. Mugwort and vervain are very complementary energies and are often used to represent the day (vervain) and night (mugwort) of either solstice. In *The Vampire Diaries*, vervain protects against vampires; this mirrors its ability to protect witches and its association with sexuality.

## Patchouli

**Botanical name:** *Pogostemon cablin*

**Element:** earth

**Astrological:** Saturn; Capricorn

**Chakra:** heart, sacral, root

**Energies:** grounding, earth magic, wealth, luxury, sensuality, attracting love, fertility, growth, sexual healing, courage

**Magical uses:** Love it or hate it, patchouli is your ultimate earth-energy herb. Both the plant and the essential oil smell like fresh earth, making patchouli perfect for grounding and growth. Patchouli is common in love and sensuality spells, but is only effective if both people enjoy the scent.

# Herbs & Greens in Practice

# Van Van Oil

This oil blend is one of the most versatile you'll come across in your practice. This hoodoo formula works for general banishing, opening, clearing, attracting, manifesting, and anointing. You name it, and Van does it. The name *Van* actually comes from *vervain*, though the plant itself is rarely included in the recipe anymore. I like to add a small piece of dried vervain to the bottle as tribute to its traditional name.

**You will need:**

- 3 ounces sweet almond oil
- 9 drops lemongrass essential oil
- 7 drops citronella essential oil
- glass bottle
- small piece dried vervain
- vetivert, palmarosa, gingergrass, and vitamin E oils and pyrite crystal (optional)

1. Combine the sweet almond oil with the lemongrass and citronella essential oils in a clean glass bottle. Add more or less of each oil based on your own preference.

2. Add a piece of dried vervain, screw on the lid, and shake your mixture well.

   Optional: The original formula included vetivert, palmarosa, and gingergrass oils from ornamental grasses, but they have become difficult to find and are very expensive. You can also add a dried piece of each herb to include the energy of the plants. Vitamin E oil acts as a preservative for carrier and essential oils, so I like to add a few drops to every blend I make. A commercial blend of Van Van oil from Lucky Mojo Curio Co. includes a small piece of pyrite and a lemongrass leaf, and those are also great additions.

# Psychic Hangover Tea

New and experienced psychics alike can come down with a psychic hangover after stretching that particular muscle for too long. This special and restorative tea blend includes energizing black tea along with herbs for clearing the mind and relaxation. This recipe will make quite a few cups of tea so you can always have some on hand when you need it. It can be made hot in the moment or brewed in a teapot, iced, and saved for later.

## You will need:

- teapot
- 6 teaspoons black tea
- 2 teaspoons rose hips
- 2 teaspoons chamomile
- 2 teaspoons mint
- 1 teaspoon lavender
- metal tea ball or fillable tea bags
- your favorite teacup and saucer
- tin or bag for storage
- honey or sugar, milk, and ice (optional)

1. Combine your herbs, and add a rounded teaspoon to your tea ball or bag for every cup of hot water.

2. Let your tea steep for three minutes and then give it a taste. If you like, you can add more tea leaves or water, honey or sugar for sweetening, or milk. Take time to enjoy your tea.

3. Now that you have a nice cup of witchy tea brewed, it would be a shame not to look at the leaves. Leave your tea leaves loose in the cup while you sip, being sure not to drink any. When you've got just a sip left, hold the cup in your left hand and ask your question. Invert the cup onto the saucer, spinning the cup around so the handle is on the right. After a minute or so, pick up your cup and look for symbols like animals, numbers, mythical creatures, letters, and meaningful objccts to deduce the message.

# Herbal Healing Salve

This is a salve for physical healing that's particularly good for all manner of witchy wounds, such as cuts, bruises, dry skin, chapped lips, headaches, bug bites, and stings.

Before you make the salve, you'll have to infuse your olive oil and your herbs.

Magically speaking, this salve contains magical flowers and herbs that are all very protective and healing and work together to balance all the chakras. They also have the element of travel magic and protection, so this is one to take on vacation.

**You will need:**

- 1 ounce dried herbs—equal parts comfrey leaf, calendula flowers, plantain, and St. John's wort
- small kitchen scale (optional)
- 16-ounce mason jar
- 1 cup extra-virgin olive oil
- cheesecloth and strainer
- 1 ounce beeswax chunk
- double boiler or saucepan
- wooden spoon
- glass measuring cup
- 15 to 20 drops essential oil of lavender, tea tree, or citronella (or a combination)
- glass jars (2 to 4 ounces) or aluminum tins (1 ounce) for storage
- vitamin E oil (optional)

1. Combine the dried comfrey leaf, calendula flowers, plantain, and St. John's wort together until you have one ounce of dried herbs. It's best to use a small kitchen scale for this. Add the herbs to the mason jar and slowly pour the olive oil over the top until it reaches the rim of the jar. Make sure all the herbs are saturated, and then close the jar and place it in a sunny window for anywhere between 3 and 6 weeks.

2. Strain the oil and herb mixture through a strainer lined with cheesecloth and squeeze any remaining liquid from the herbs. While this can be used as is, we will use it as the base for our salve.

3. Melt the beeswax in a double boiler or saucepan on very low heat, making sure not to burn it; you just want to melt it. Once the beeswax has melted, pour your oil in and let it warm up for a while so that it all blends together, stirring with the wooden spoon. Carefully transfer the mixture to a glass measuring cup.

4. Pour in 15 to 20 drops of an antiseptic essential oil like lavender, tea tree, or citronella and give it a quick stir.

5. Pour your salve into jars or tins for storage and to let it harden. The salve should last 6 to 9 months or up to a year if you add vitamin E to your oil blend.

# Lucky Moon Rabbit's Foot

Bring a fake lucky rabbit's foot back to life by invoking the legendary moon rabbit, which is busy blending the elixir of life in his mortar and pestle for the moon goddess. This method adds magical energy to this kitschy trinket without hurting any rabbits.

**You will need:**

- a fake rabbit's foot or fake fur to make your own
- scissors
- dried basil, patchouli, and alfalfa
- a small piece of moonstone
- fabric glue or needle and thread
- cotton batting, a piece of jade, and naturally shed rabbit fur (optional)

1. You've no doubt heard of the Man in the Moon, but in some cultures around the world, it's actually a rabbit people see on the face of the full moon. Rabbits are smart, fast, and lucky, and they always know when it's time to ground.

2. Use the scissors to make a hole in the side of the rabbit's foot that's wide enough to pull out some of the cotton batting to make room for your herbs and crystal.

3. Add a pinch of each of the herbs, one at a time, while focusing on its purpose in the spell.

   - Basil is for luck, love, and magic.

   - Patchouli is for grounding and luxury.

   - Alfalfa, the rabbit's herb, is for good luck and to make sure you never go hungry.

4. Place the moonstone inside as well to bring in the healing and magical energy of the moon, and glue or sew up the hole when you're finished. Carry this just like you would a lucky rabbit's foot, especially while traveling.

   Optional: In China, the moon rabbit was also called the jade rabbit, and since jade is a stone of good fortune, it's a great addition to this spell. If you have a pet rabbit, you can collect a small amount of fur that comes out from brushing your pet, but you'll want to ask them first.

# Nightingale Candle Spell for Quick Healing

Named after the pioneer of modern nursing, this candle is meant to soothe and heal anyone recovering from illness, injury, or heartbreak.

This is a classic candle spell method that can be adapted for any purpose by changing the color of the candle and the types of herbs and oils used. Burn this candle in the room with the person healing for a little while every day. If it's a long illness, you can get a really large seven-day candle, or you can make this with a votive or taper if you need it quickly.

**You will need:**

- white pillar candle
- something to carve a candle with, like a nail or toothpick
- Van Van or other dressing oil
- pinch dried bladderwrack
- pinch dried motherwort
- glass candleholder

1. Carve the name of the person the candle is for on one side of the candle from base to wick and then down the other side.

2. Place a few drops of Van Van oil (or a bit of the oil from your healing salve) into your hand and cover the candle going upward on one side and down the other. This creates a cycle of moving energy so that nothing can stagnate, since Van Van clears out and unblocks.

3. Sprinkle a light pinch of both bladderwrack and motherwort all over the candle, allowing them to lend their powers of healing and comfort, like a bowl of homemade chicken noodle soup.

4. Place the candle in a glass candleholder. Light the candle for a short time every day to speed healing and say the following invocation: "May the lady of the lamp watch over you and grant you the gifts of health and comfort."

5. Burn the candle all the way down to help clear out any lingering energy or illness. When it's finished, dispose of the remains in the trash to help get rid of the illness for good.

## Chapter Seven
# The Wisdom of Wood

Trees are vital to our survival and our spiritual development. With life spans in the thousands of years, these ancient ancestors impart on us the wisdom of the ages.

# Wood & Trees

The following 15 trees, woods, and resins mark the entrance to the world of magic.

## Birch

**Botanical name:** *Betula*

**Element:** water, fire

**Astrological:** Moon

**Celtic tree zodiac:** December 24–January 20

**Energies:** growth, renewal, creativity, protection, new beginnings, attracting, initiation, spirituality, writing, record keeping

**Magical uses:** The birch is first on the Celtic tree calendar and symbolizes renewal, new beginnings, and protection. Birch twigs and branches are used to make brooms and altar decor, and the wood is burned to bring prosperity to us in the new year. The thin bark of the birch tree resembles paper and can be used for writing spells and invocations.

## Oak

**Botanical name:** *Quercus*

**Element:** earth

**Astrological:** Sun

**Celtic tree zodiac:** June 10–July 7

**Energies:** divination, manifestation, healing, victory, prosperity, strength, Druidry, responsibility, faerie magic

Magical uses: The mighty oak tree is considered the father of all trees and the forest. In modern Druidic practice, the oak tree is the most sacred tree. Oaks grow in groves, which are said to host clandestine magical meetings with humans and faeries alike. Acorns are carried as talismans for protection and fertility and to encourage the growth of prosperity over many years.

## Frankincense

**Botanical name:** *Boswellia sacra*

**Element:** air, fire

**Astrological:** Sun

**Energies:** purification, protection, meditation, exorcism, spiritual development, happiness, wealth, spiritual celebration

Magical uses: Frankincense is resin-based incense from the Boswellia tree and has been harvested and traded for thousands of years. Many people know of frankincense as one of the gifts brought to the baby Jesus by the Magi, or Wise Men. Today, it is still used for spiritual development, protection, and purification and as a blessing. The tree that produces this resin is in the same family as myrrh (another biblical gift), copal, and palo santo, all of which are heavily featured in spiritual practices around the world.

## Horse Chestnut/Buckeye

**Botanical name:** *Aesculus hippocastanum*

**Element:** fire

**Astrological:** Jupiter

**Energies:** harmony, money, peace, health, luck, love, lust, hope, longevity, intuition, grounding, the autumn equinox, safety

**Magical uses:** This beautiful tree isn't a true chestnut, so don't go roasting the fruit on an open fire.* Around the autumn equinox, the horse chestnut drops large seeds wrapped in spiky seed pods called buckeyes, which are carried and hung as talismans for luck, love, and attraction. The tree has become a symbol of safety and comfort at home and the undying hope that the future will be better.

*The fruit of the horse chestnut can make you sick if ingested but is safe to touch.

## Maple

**Botanical name:** *Acer saccharum*

**Element:** air

**Astrological:** Jupiter, Neptune

**Energies:** attraction, sweetness, love, strength, athletic achievement, energy, flying, travel, change, prosperity, strength, music, positivity

**Magical uses:** There are more than 100 varieties of maple out there, but the variety most commonly referred to and used is the sugar maple, the source of maple syrup and the symbol of Canada. Maple leaves can be used in magic to attract money and prosperity, the branches can be made into wands, the seeds carried as talismans, and the sap made into syrup, which has all of these magical properties synthesized into it with the added energy of attraction.

# Redwood/Sequoia

Botanical name: *Sequoioideae*

Element: fire

Astrological: Jupiter

Energies: abundance, prosperity, wisdom, longevity, immortality, growth, earth magic, balance, spiritual advancement, innovation, spiritual connection, protection

Magical uses: The gigantic redwoods of northern California are the largest trees in the world and can live for thousands of years. The wood makes beautiful wands, while the cherry-shaped pine cones can be used as talismans or ingredients in herbal blends. The redwood's ability to reach seemingly all the way into the cosmos makes it a beautiful ally in spiritual development and connection.

# Pine

Botanical name: *Pinus*

Element: fire, air

Astrological: Saturn

Energies: spiritual cleansing, wisdom, abundance, health, fertility, fortune, love, health, protection, warmth and comfort, celebration, the winter solstice, harmony with nature

Magical uses: The indigenous peoples of North America all recognized the pine as an important tree, and though the actual associations vary from tribe to tribe, it's seen as a symbol of protection, spirituality, and wisdom. Pine branches and needles can be added to incense or smoke cleansing bundles, while pine cones can be burned in bonfires or carried as talismans of health and fertility.

## Ash

**Botanical name:** *Fraxinus*

**Element:** aether, all others

**Astrological:** Neptune, Sun

**Celtic tree zodiac:** February 18–March 17

**Energies:** the world tree, love, prosperity, protection, justice, dream magic, strength, harmony with nature, birth, faerie magic, connection with other worlds

**Magical uses:** Ash is the traditional choice for the handle of a witch's broom because of its strength and connection with the whole of the universe. As the world tree, the ash connects us with nature, the cosmos, the living, the dead, and the magical.

## Willow

**Botanical name:** *Salix Alba*

**Element:** water

**Astrological:** Moon

**Celtic tree zodiac:** April 15–May 12

**Energies:** lunar magic, healing, pain relief, meditation, magic, creativity, inspiration, love, tranquility, growth, renewal, mediumship, safety, dream magic, mental clarity, enchantment, divination, binding

**Magical uses:** Another sacred tree from the time of the Druids, the willow is the ultimate symbol of the moon here on earth. White willow bark is used to create aspirin, and its magical uses include mental clarity, healing, and pain relief to mirror that. Thick willow branches are popular for wands, while the wispy branches are used to bind the bristles of a broom.

## Dragon's Blood

**Botanical name:** *Dracaena cinnabari*, *Dracaena draco*

**Element:** fire

**Astrological:** Mars, Jupiter

**Energies:** protection, good fortune, activation, cleansing, hex breaking, manifestation, love, passion

**Magical uses:** Dragon's blood is, of course, not really the blood of a dragon. This is a resin from a few different species of tree native to northern Africa and the Arabian Peninsula that produce a bright red sap. The resin can be used in chunks, as a powder, or in inks and oils. It's a powerful activator and good for both banishing and attracting.

## Palo Santo

**Botanical name:** *Bursera graveolens*

**Element:** air, fire

**Astrological:** Mercury

**Energies:** spiritual cleansing, banishing spirits, meditation, spiritual connection, creativity, luck, passion, healing

**Magical uses:** Palo santo, or holy wood, is native to Peru and is in the same family as frankincense, myrrh, and copal resins. It's considered a holy tree to the Incas and other South American indigenous peoples. The wood is usually burned like a cleansing wand or in incense blends, but you can also add the oil to baths and candles. To preserve the sanctity and supply of the palo santo tree, only naturally fallen wood should be harvested. The wood is usually stored for around four years so its fragrant oil can come to the surface.

## Yew

**Botanical name:** *Taxus baccata, T. brevifolia, T. canadensis*

**Element:** aether, all other elements

**Astrological:** Saturn, Pluto

**Energies:** hallowed ground, death, rebirth, transformation, ancestors, wisdom, mediumship, dream magic, psychic power, divination, the winter solstice

**Magical uses:** Perhaps because of its toxicity or its association with immortality, yew is a popular tree in graveyards and church-yards in the British Isles. It's burned both to banish spirits of the dead and to facilitate communication with them, as the yew tree straddles both worlds. The wood of the yew tree is safe to work with and is used to make archery bows, wands, and a set of divination tools called Ogham staves.

## Apple

**Botanical name:** *Malus*

**Element:** water, aether

**Astrological:** Venus

**Energies:** love, divination, freedom, women's empowerment, abundance, blessings, healing, the elements, knowledge, wisdom, death, fertility, magic, the autumn equinox, Samhain, attraction, blessings, beauty

**Magical uses:** Apple is the traditional wood for the witch's wand, as it's seen as a true symbol of magic. The fruit of the tree has been provocative for thousands of years as the fruit of the dead, knowledge, the gods, life, blessing, and curses. Apples have also been popular tools for love divination. On Halloween, eat a fresh apple in front of the mirror at midnight to see the face of your future love, or peel the skin from an apple in a spiral and throw it over your right shoulder. The peel should spell the first initial of your future love.

## Fig

**Botanical name:** *Ficus religiosa, F. carica*

**Element:** aether

**Astrological:** Neptune, Saturn

**Energies:** enlightenment, fertility, healing, weather magic, wisdom, protection, grounding, divination, sexuality, love, wisdom

**Magical uses:** The fig is another tree and fruit associated with wisdom and divine knowledge. The sacred fig in India is revered, as the Buddha attained enlightenment while meditating under a large sacred fig, now known as the Bodhi tree. In the Mediterranean, the fruit of the fig tree is a symbol of love, sexuality, and fertility, and the scent and flavor of figs are common in love potions and spells.

# Sandalwood

**Botanical name:** *Santalum album*

**Element:** water

**Astrological:** Moon

**Energies:** love, past lives, protection, healing, sensuality, beauty, meditation, wishes, spiritual cleansing, enlightenment, grounding

**Magical uses:** The lovely fragrance of sandalwood is welcome in spiritual spaces around the world. It's burned as a sacred incense, and the oil is used to consecrate objects as well as in baths and perfumes. The wood is often carved into beads and used to make malas, or strings of prayer beads, for meditation. This white wood is associated with the moon and its calming spiritual energy.

# Wood & Trees in Practice

# Sacred Tree Incense

Mixing your incense blends is a really creative and rewarding way to work with magical trees and herbs. It's a very intuitive process, and the exact quantities of each item will depend on what you like or need more of.

**You will need:**

- frankincense resin
- dragon's blood resin
- mortar and pestle
- mixing bowl
- white willow bark shavings
- palo santo shavings
- bark or resin from your Celtic zodiac tree (optional)
- sandalwood essential oil
- matches
- charcoal disc and fireproof dish
- mason jar for storage

1. Put a small amount of each of the resins in your mortar and use the pestle to lightly crush them together so you have a coarse powder.

2. Add white willow bark shavings to your bowl. This wood doesn't have a lot of fragrance while burned, so you can use as much as you like. This is a sacred tree of the moon.

3. Add palo santo shavings to the bowl, but remember that this wood *is* very fragrant. It has a beautiful, fiery scent that burns away anything that's not meant to be there.

4. Bark or resin from your Celtic zodiac tree can be added to personalize the incense blend.

5. Sprinkle your powdered resins over the willow and palo santo, and add extra whole chunks as well. Sprinkle five drops of sandalwood oil and blend it all together.

6. Burn your incense by holding a match to a self-lighting charcoal disc until the heat is evenly dispersed. Put a small amount of the incense onto the disc, and watch the smoke rise from your bowl. A little goes a long way, so store the rest in a mason jar for future acts of magic or meditation.

# If the Broom Fits, Ride It

Once you find a good piece of ash for the handle of your broom, it's surprisingly easy to make. When you're finished, you can leave the broom *au naturel* or decorate it with anything you can imagine.

**You will need:**

- large handful of broomcorn
- long length of willow
- large tub of hot water
- ash wood (4 feet long, 2 inches thick)
- roll of hemp twine
- scissors
- beeswax, oils, paint, wood-burning or carving tools, colored string or ribbon, fresh herb branches, charms and beads, flowers and vines, birch twigs, and dragon's blood ink (optional)

1. Soak your broomcorn and length of willow in a tub of hot water overnight to make them pliable.

2. Lay your ash wood handle out on a large flat surface. Cut a piece of hemp twine the length of your forearm and another the length of your whole arm, and put them aside.

3. Line up your broomcorn about four inches from the bottom of your handle with the bottom facing the top of the broom. (You'll be bending them the other way.) Tightly fasten the bristles to the staff with the shorter length of hemp twine.

4. Carefully bend the broomcorn toward the bottom end of the broom and fasten it tightly around the same place with the longer piece of twine. Wrap your length of willow around the outside of the twine and tie it tightly to seal in your intentions.

5. Decorate your broom as you wish once it's fully dry. You can seal up the wood of the handle with melted beeswax to preserve. If you'd like to learn more about using your broom, check out *The Witch's Broom* by Deborah Blake.

# The Ace of Wands

The most difficult part of making your own wand is finding a suitable branch, which could take hours or even weeks of walking through wooded areas. Apple is the most common wood for wands, but you can use any tree that grows in your local area. You and your natural environment are linked, and that extends to the trees.

**You will need:**

- paper and pen
- sacred tree
- incense and charcoal for burning
- sturdy branch from a magical tree like apple or willow, naturally fallen
- knife
- sandpaper
- beeswax, oils, colored strings or ribbons, glue, crystals, beads and charms, and fabric (optional)

1. Plan a day when you can go for a walk or hike to search for wood for your wand, and remember to check local laws and poison warnings.

2. Think about what kind of wand you want to make or what purpose you need it for. Write down your thoughts on a small square of paper, and fold the paper into a smaller square.

3. Light some of your sacred tree incense and place your note on top. Open your window or go outside with your incense, and imagine your wishes being carried out to all the trees in the area. Waft the smoke around you to cleanse your aura and keep the energy of your intention on you.

4. Focus on your wishes for a wand, and let your intuition guide you to a naturally fallen branch.

5. Clean and trim it up, and sand down any rough edges. You can remove the bark if you like, but your wand can look however you like. If you'd like to seal it up to protect the wood, melt a small amount of beeswax and carefully rub it into the wand with a soft cloth.

6. If you choose to decorate your wand, feel free to do so with fabric, charms and beads, magical inks and paints, wood-burned symbols, or crystals.

7. Light more of your sacred tree incense. Wave your finished wand through the smoke and use it to surround yourself with the smoke again. You and your wand are linked.

Note: This is the most basic way to make a wand, but if you have any carpentry skills, feel free to break out your lathe and stains and sealants. If you'd like to learn more about your wand, check out *The Witch's Wand* by Alferian Gwydion MacLir.

# Maple Syrup Sweetening Spell

This slight twist on the classic hoodoo honey jar features maple syrup to sweeten someone to you—a lover, an employer, a customer, or maybe a potential landlord.

Since maple is so multipurpose, this spell can be used for any of the purposes listed earlier in the chapter. If you're working to attract a lover, use a red or pink candle and rose petals, a picture, or a lock of hair. For a job, a green or gold candle is best, and add glitter or magical money, a business card for the place to which you're applying to work, or other magical money talismans like sequoia pine cones.

**You will need:**

- 4-ounce glass jar with metal lid
- pure maple syrup
- square of paper and pen
- personal concerns like photos, locks of hair, or a business card (optional)
- herbs, roots, flower petals, coins, and glitter (optional)
- taper candle and appropriate dressing oil

1. Fill your jar almost to the rim with maple syrup and set it aside.

2. Write your name, the name of the one you want to sweeten to you, and your intentions in a specific pattern on your piece of paper.

   - Write the name of the one you wish to sweeten three times in the middle of the paper.

   - Rotate the paper 90 degrees clockwise, and write your name so it covers the other. You want it to look like a hashtag shape (or tic-tac-toe).

   - Write your intention in a circle around the name you've written without lifting your pen from the paper until the two ends meet. Don't dot the i's or cross the t's, and don't add spaces.

   - Fold the paper in half toward you, spin it 90 degrees clockwise, and fold it again. Follow this until you have a small square.

3. Dip your finger in the jar and take a taste of the maple syrup, relishing the sweetness. Put your petition paper into the jar and make sure it's covered with syrup. Add any extra herbs or supplies, photos (they will be ruined), or business cards, as you wish. When everything is inside, close the jar tightly.

4. Dress your candle with whatever oil you're using in an upward motion, and then melt the bottom of the candle a little so you can stick it onto the lid. Keep your intention in your mind and light the candle. If the spell hasn't finished by the time the candle burns down, feel free to light another one.

# Willow Tree Full Moon Meditation

Not every tree has to be chopped down, burned, bled, or pulverized for you to connect with its energy for magic. You can also connect on a regular basis with the living tree just by making contact and opening your mind.

On the night of a full moon, find a willow tree in your yard or a public place that you can sit under without being disturbed. Make sure you can see the moon through the branches. You can bring a blanket or pillow to make you more comfortable, but try to make contact with the roots or trunk.

The elemental grounding exercise you've been perfecting over the last few chapters connects you with the four physical elements, and now you're going to be reaching out to the fifth one—aether or spirit. This is the element of magic, spirituality, and the cosmos.

Get comfortable, and begin by connecting to the

physical elements. Hear the breeze blowing through the willow's graceful branches, feel the shelter of its warm embrace, and imagine the water in the earth being drawn to the surface by the force of the moon. Feel the stability of the earth below you and the strength of the willow's roots. As the moon pulls the water up to feed the tree's roots, the willow is pulling the moonlight down to earth to make everything around you grow lush. You're a part of this cycle now too. Imagine the light of the moon dripping down from every willow branch, surrounding you in its light. This is the element of the spirit.

How does it feel? Is it like any of the other elements?

Take some time to look at the moon, and stay as long as you'd like. If you'd like to collect willow branches for wands of brooms, this would be the perfect time.

If you don't have access to a real willow, this meditation can still be done with a little extra imagination. You can also find a photo or video of a willow tree that speaks to you and makes you feel calm.

### Chapter Eight

# The Strength of Stones & Crystals

Stones, crystals, and magic rocks—these strong, glittering pieces of earth magic can put us in touch with the ancient wisdom of the planet.

# Crystals

There are hundreds of varieties of beautiful and powerful crystals out there, but the following 15 are especially suited for the practice of green witchcraft.

**Warning:** Some of the crystals listed in this chapter, such as malachite, moonstone, and chrysocolla, either can be damaged by water or can leach toxic metal into water and should never be submerged. Always do your research.

## Quartz

**Other name:** the master healer

**Type of mineral:** silicon dioxide

**Element:** aether

**Astrological:** Aries, Leo

**Chakra:** crown, third eye, throat, heart, solar plexus, sacral, root

**Energies:** all-purpose, healing, attraction, banishing, manifestation, new beginnings, protection, cleansing, chakra balancing, meditation

**Magical uses:** Clear quartz is the ultimate multipurpose crystal and can be used to project or bring in any kind of energy. It can also stand in for any stone. It's known as the master healer both spiritually and emotionally.

## Amethyst

**Type of mineral:** silicon dioxide, manganese

**Element:** water

**Astrological:** Aquarius, Pisces

**Chakra:** third eye, crown

**Energies:** intuition, comfort, sleep, safe travel, manifestation, overcoming addiction and maintaining sobriety, protection from negative energy and spirits, love

**Magical uses:** This purple variety of quartz is often called the lavender of crystals because of its universal appeal and calming energy. Amethyst can help you get more restful sleep with fewer nightmares and open your mind to new thoughts and meditation.

## Moonstone

**Other name:** rainbow moonstone

**Type of Mineral:** feldspar

**Element:** water

**Astrological:** Moon, Cancer

**Chakra:** sacral, third eye, crown

**Energies:** intuition, meditation, full moon magic, psychic power, mental clarity, creativity, self-expression, travel protection, women's health, empowerment

**Magical uses:** There are a few varieties of moonstone, but the rainbow one is the most beautiful and powerful. This crystal is a solid representation of the bright, shining full moon. It's intuitive, healing, and mysterious. It's a talisman for traveling in the dark, across water, or anywhere you might need the moon to light the way.

## Labradorite

**Type of mineral:** plagioclase feldspar

**Element:** water

**Astrological:** Scorpio

**Chakra:** third eye, throat

**Energies:** intuition, meditation, new moon magic, dispelling illusion, clairvoyance, independence, the aurora borealis, communication

**Magical uses:** If the white/rainbow variety of feldspar is the full moon, labradorite is the new moon showing only a fleeting sliver of light. It's a stone of intuition, meditation, and mental clarity. The luminescent colors of the labradorite were considered to be the aurora borealis synthesized into a stone by the indigenous peoples of the Atlantic Canada.

## Moss & Tree Agate

**Type of mineral:** quartz with manganese and iron (moss); and chalcedony with dendrite (tree)

**Element:** earth

**Astrological:** Virgo

**Chakra:** heart (moss), earth star (tree)

Energies: moss—stone of gardeners, new beginnings, growth, lucky, drawing in business, animal magic, entrepreneurship, and prosperity; tree—abundance, growth, healing the earth, connections, clearing blockages, tree magic

Magical uses: Though these stones are made up of slightly different minerals, their overall energy is so complementary that they act like sister stones. Both focus on drawing in prosperity and abundance and connecting us to the energies of the earth. While moss agate gently connects us to the deep energy of the fresh earth, tree agate reminds us that the sky, or canopy, is the limit. These stones are the ultimate green witch crystal combination.

## Obsidian

Other name: the wizard stone

Type of mineral: volcanic glass, magma

Element: all

Astrological: Scorpio

Chakra: root

Energies: emotional healing, absorbing negative energy, cleansing, harmony, protection, confidence, scrying, divination, personal power, animal magic, grounding

Magical uses: Obsidian is protective, healing, and grounding. This volcanic glass is carried and worn for personal power, displayed in the heart of your home to harmonize the energy, and used for scrying and divination.

## Malachite

**Type of mineral:** copper carbonite

**Element:** earth

**Astrological:** Scorpio

**Chakra:** heart

**Energies:** protection, love, enchantment, healing from trauma, sensuality, encouraging healthy relationships, bravery, travel magic, conquering fear, absorbing energy

**Magical uses:** In its raw form, malachite can be toxic and shouldn't be in contact with the skin for long. Luckily, when it's tumbled, it's safe to carry and wear because this stone is really something special. In ancient Egypt, the sarcophagi of pharaohs featured a carved malachite heart to ensure theirs would make it to the afterlife safe and sound.

## Bloodstone

**Other name:** heliotrope

**Type of mineral:** jasper chalcedony

**Element:** earth, fire

**Astrological:** Aries

**Chakra:** root, sacral, heart

**Energies:** healing families, athletic ability, energy, protection, wealth, earth magic, good luck, grounding, creativity, ancestors

**Magical uses:** Bloodstone was the first crystal I ever bought and worked with, and to this day, it's one of my favorites. It's warm and comforting as well as passionate and protective. It's great for grounding, prosperity magic, and increasing your physical stamina and athletic abilities. It's also the stone of family drama and healing. Bloodstone can help you heal from a difficult family situation, help you connect more with family heart to heart, and heal spiritual trauma passed down through the generations.

## Rose Quartz

Type of mineral: silicon dioxide, manganese

Element: water

Astrological: Taurus

Chakra: heart

Energies: compassion, romance, self-love, emotional healing, fun, sweetness, peace, beauty, forgiveness, self-care

Magical uses: The ultimate stone of gentle, unconditional love, this sweet stone can be given to others so they can always feel your heart with them, and it can also heal a broken heart or a broken relationship. It's a strong stone of the self.

## Lava Stone & Pumice

Type of mineral: volcanic rock

Element: all

Astrological: Aries, Scorpio

Chakra: solar plexus, sacral

Energies: energy, fire, harmony, protection, lucky, emotional healing, harmony, stamina, cleansing, beauty

Magical uses: Lava stone and pumice are both formed during volcanic eruptions, when the volcanic rock begins to cool, but pumice has more gases and air trapped in it than the black lava stone. The energy of all four physical elements went into their creation, making them a great grounding tool. Though they're both associated with the fiery passion of Pele the Hawaiian volcano goddess, they're also connected to the cleansing power of the ocean.

## Galaxyite

Other name: galaxite

Type of mineral: micro feldspar

Element: aether

Astrological: Sagittarius

Chakra: crown

Energies: aura cleansing, healing, and energizing, aura reading, astrology, wonderment, other galaxies, cosmic beings, astral travel, soothing, intergalactic communication, dream magic, spirituality, mental clarity

Magical uses: This is another variety of feldspar like moonstone and labradorite, but the smaller flecks make this stone sparkle like a sky full of stars. It's a stone of power for astrologers and astronomers, stargazers, UFO hunters, and aura readers. It's the ultimate crystal for cleansing and repairing the auric field, making it very soothing to hold in times of anxiety or pain.

## Aquamarine

**Type of mineral:** beryl

**Element:** water

**Astrological:** Pisces

**Chakra:** throat, heart, third eye

**Energies:** water magic, beauty, love spells, healing, intuition, attraction, good luck, mermaid magic, justice, humbleness, quiet courage, antianxiety, travel magic, calming, self-expression, going with the flow

**Magical uses:** Aquamarine is known as a mermaid stone and the crystal version of the spirit of the ocean. It's associated with beauty, love, and intuition and is an excellent stone to carry with you daily. When life is chaotic and you're struggling to stay afloat, carry aquamarine and obsidian together. This harnesses the energy of both the exploding volcano and the deep ocean to keep you balanced and steady while going through change.

## Aragonite

**Type of mineral:** dimorphous calcium carbonate

**Element:** earth, water

**Astrological:** Capricorn

**Chakra:** earth star, sacral, root

**Energies:** earth spirituality, healing relationships, healing the earth, grounding, moderation, success, feeling at home in your body, connections, balancing the material and magical, generosity, patience

**Magical uses:** This stone is a rusty-orange color reminiscent of the orange clay of the Appalachian Mountain Range. It grows in sparkling clusters that end not in points but in blunt little mirrors. Aragonite connects you with the energy of the earth in a very deep way and can help you connect to your own wild nature.

## Chrysocolla

**Type of mineral:** hydrated copper silicate, chalcedony quartz

**Element:** earth

**Astrological:** Taurus, Libra

**Chakra:** heart, throat

**Energies:** tranquility, communication, supporting feminine energies in all people, emotional protection, joy, wisdom, comfort for those living alone, music, maturity, blocks unwanted communication, sensuality, women's independence, meditation, honesty

**Magical uses:** Chrysocolla is reminiscent of turquoise but features darker tones of blue and green along with the lighter color. This stone is associated with strong women who feel confident at any age and those of any gender presentation who want to connect to energy considered feminine in a safe and supported way. It's calming and tranquil and both helps you communicate better and keeps you from having to communicate with those who won't do you any good.

# Himalayan Salt

**Other name:** pink halite

**Type of mineral:** halide, sodium chloride

**Element:** earth

**Astrological:** Cancer, Pisces

**Chakra:** heart, sacral

**Energies:** self-love, protection, cleansing, love, grounding, health, success, starting over, happiness, healing relationships and broken hearts, purification

**Magical uses:** There are a lot of varieties of salt out there, and they're all useful in your magical practice for cleansing and grounding, but pink Himalayan salt is all the rage, and with good reason. This beautiful mineral in shades of pink and orange is a fantastic cleanser of the body and home and for the spiritual space around us. It can be found in large chunks as a crystal specimen or coarsely ground for culinary uses and health reasons.

# Stones & Crystals in Practice

# Galaxyite Aura Cleanse

Galaxyite is the ultimate crystal to help care for your aura by cleansing and repairing your energy field.

**You will need:**

- 1 piece of galaxyite, tumbled or carved into a wand

1.  In a quiet room, take your galaxyite in your dominant hand and hold it above your crown, a few inches from your physical body.

2.  Slowly comb the stone downward, making note of any sensations you feel. Brush down your head, face, arms, chest, legs, and even feet. If you feel like any part of your aura needs more attention, hold the crystal there and imagine its starry inclusions forming a patch that blends with your aura.

Note: You can also use this crystal to help you see or read auras more clearly and to gain greater understanding in other cosmic areas of knowledge, like astrology.

# Crystal Grid for Courage

This crystal grid will give you a beacon of safety and support to return to whenever you feel overwhelmed by your fears. Build this crystal grid on your altar in the shape of a square, which is a symbol of strong boundaries, grounding, and increased confidence.

**You will need:**

- 4 pieces obsidian

- ½ cup coarsely ground Himalayan salt

- square crystal grid template or plate (optional)

- 4 pieces bloodstone

- 1 large piece malachite

- piece of paper and pen

- your wand, more crystals, herbs or flowers associated with courage and bravery (optional)

1.  Gather your items at your altar or workspace, and start by focusing on your intention. If there's nothing specific you need, start with, "I am safe, I am strong, and my heart knows no fear."

2.  Collect your four pieces of obsidian for the outer perimeter of your grid to harness its incredible protective energy. Place one in each corner of your square. Use your salt to draw a line connecting each of the obsidian pieces to cleanse your space of any incoming negative energy. You can also use a square crystal grid template or plate for guidance if you like.

3. Make a smaller square inside that boundary with your bloodstones on the four corners. This grounding stone is associated with families and ancestors, so this can symbolize keeping your family safe or counting on your family to make you feel safe (or both).

4. Place your malachite in the middle, as this is the focus stone of this grid. Malachite is an intense stone associated with both healing the heart and conquering fear. It's also slightly toxic in its raw form, which adds another layer of protection. Set your intention paper in the middle of the grid with the malachite on top.

5. Add any other crystals, herbs, or other items you wish to your grid to personalize it, but do it without breaking that outer perimeter of salt and obsidian.

6. Activate the grid using your wand or finger to touch each main crystal moving from your boundary into your safe and snug malachite heart stone. Touch the obsidian and say, "I am safe." Touch the bloodstones and say, "I am/My family is strong." Finally, touch the malachite and say, "My heart knows no fear." Meditate with your grid whenever you need extra courage.

# Aquamarine Crystal Elixir

Crystal elixirs and essences are the spirit and energy of crystals suspended in water. This aquamarine elixir can be added to beverages, baths, and meals or taken under the tongue whenever you want to harness magical mermaid energy.

**You will need:**

- 1 tumbled piece aquamarine
- spring water
- clean, clear glass jar
- small dropper or spray bottle (or many)
- alcohol—brandy or vodka works well

1. Clean your aquamarine under running water. Gently place the crystal at the bottom of the jar and cover it with as much water as you'd like.

2. Put the jar in a window where the sun can shine directly on it for 3 to 4 hours. Make sure shade never touches your jar.

3. Use your intuition to determine when your elixir is ready to use. I know mine is ready when the jar has very tiny bubbles clinging to the sides and the water starts to take on a rainbow color or energy.

4. Preserve your elixir by transferring it to dropper bottles, filling each three-quarters of the way. Fill the bottle the rest of the way with vodka or brandy to keep the water from going stale.

   Note: Aquamarine is great for a starter elixir because it's safe, clean, and already so aligned with water. Since it's a crystal of beauty, aquamarine elixir can be added to a face mist (like the one made from red clover in chapter 4) or perfume.

# Connect to Your Earth Star Chakra

The seven bodily chakras we've explored in this book are the most well known, but our bodies are actually full of thousands of these magical energy centers. After the chakras of the physical body come those of the spiritual body. The most important of these for green witches to connect to is called the earth star chakra, which is located under the earth's surface. Think of the earth star as the tether holding you not only to the physical planet but also to the magical energy, humans, and creatures who live here.

Orange aragonite is a beautiful crystal for connecting to this earth energy, and I often imagine the chakra itself looking like a sparkly aragonite cluster.

Stand or sit with your feet flat on the ground; it's better if you're outside. Place an aragonite cluster between your feet, and go through your grounding meditation. Imagine this rust-colored star sitting a foot below the earth. Visualize thin, golden threads rising up through the earth and connecting to each one of your feet. Trust that if you ever get disconnected from the earth's energy and start to float away or forget your place in the world, those golden threads are gently anchoring you to your crystal chakra.

When you're consciously connected to the earth star, you can bring energy up from the earth more easily and send healing energy back into it. This chakra can help you understand the ways you can serve or save the earth and its inhabitants, how you can contribute to the cycles of nature, and how you can use your powers of green witch-craft to make a difference in the world.

# Crystal Plant Medicine

Thinking of growing your own magical plants to use in your practice? This quick spell features moss and tree agate to help initiate them into magic and strengthen your connection. This spell can be done either before or after you've planted and at any growing stage.

**You will need:**

- potted plant or seeds
- 1 piece tumbled tree agate
- 1 piece tumbled moss agate

1. Place one hand in the soil you're using while holding the agate pieces to your heart.

2. Imagine or feel a green light growing around the crystal and your heart, connecting them.

3. Move in close to your plant (or seeds) and say:

   *As I grow, so will you.*

   *As I flourish, so will you.*

   *As I open to the magic of the earth, so will you.*

   *As I love, I'll love you too.*

4. Bury the crystals in the soil, and imagine your plant by its roots, making it strong and healthy.

# Conclusion

With this practical guide to green witchcraft, I hope that you've found yourself at the beginning of a fresh, new path: a path marked with fragrant flowers and herbs, glittering crystals, towering trees and acts of magic. By immersing yourself in these pages, you've already initiated a deeper relationship with the earth right where you are—whether you're in a tiny forest cottage, or a balcony overlooking the city—that will support you no matter where your green witchcraft practice takes you.

As you go forward, creating your own path as you go, remember to remain curious and humble in the wilderness. Never forget to trust your senses, both physical and psychic, and hone your relationship to the natural, magical world that you inhabit. Remember to listen to the invaluable wisdom of our ancient arboreal ancestors. Embrace all that this sacred world has to teach you, and lean in to the feeling of the pull of the moon and the expansion of the cosmos. And last but not least, continue to connect to and nurture your unique and glittering tether that reaches the deep engine of the earth.

# Resources

Basile, Lisa Marie. *Light Magic for Dark Times: More than 100 Spells, Rituals, and Practices for Coping in a Crisis*. Beverly, MA: Fair Winds Press, 2018.

The spells and rituals in this book are the very definition of practical and accessible magic for every purpose.

Bird, Stephanie Rose. *Sticks, Stones, Roots & Bones: Hoodoo, Mojo & Conjuring with Herbs*. Woodbury, MN: Llewellyn, 2004.

An excellent guide to the herbs, roots, and traditions of hoodoo practices.

Blackthorn, Amy. *Blackthorn's Botanical Magic: The Green Witch's Guide to Essential Oils for Spellcraft, Ritual & Healing*. Newburyport, MA: Weiser Books, 2018.

This new book tells you everything you need to know about using essential oils in your practice.

Blake, Deborah. *The Witch's Broom: The Craft, Lore & Magick of Broomsticks*. Woodbury, MN: Llewellyn, 2014.

Deborah Blake is the queen of "everyday witchcraft," and this guide provides witches with modern ways to make, decorate, and use brooms in their practice.

Dugan, Ellen. *The Natural Psychic*. Woodbury, MN: Llewellyn, 2015.

Ellen Dugan is known as "The Garden Witch" and her knowledge of plant magic is astounding! This book focuses on harnessing and nurturing your natural psychic senses.

Eason, Cassandra. *The Complete Crystal Handbook: Your Guide to More Than 500 Crystals*. New York: Sterling, 2010.

This is an encyclopedia of 500 crystals, and includes practical uses for crystals in spells, at work or at home, and in divination.

MacLir, Alferian Gwydion. *The Witch's Wand: The Craft, Lore, and Magick of Wands & Staffs* (*The Witch's Tools Series*). Woodbury, MN: Llewellyn, 2015.

This small guide by a real wand-maker features everything you could need to know about making and using your own wand, and the history behind their use in magic.

Roth, Harold. *The Witching Herbs: 13 Essential Plants and Herbs for Your Magical Garden*. Newburyport, MA: Weiser Books, 2017.

Roth has been a magical herbalist for more than 20 years and specializes in poisonous plants like Datura. He provides detailed growing and magical instructions in *The Witching Herbs* and sells seeds on his website Alchemy Works.

Smith, Jacki. *Coventry Magic with Candles, Oils, and Herbs*. Newburyport, MA: Weiser Books, 2011.

This hoodoo-inspired book is an incredible guide for getting started on a witchy path and working with candles, but it's also inspiring and empowering.

Whitehurst, Tess. *The Magic of Flowers: A Guide to Their Metaphysical Uses & Properties*. Woodbury, MN: Llewellyn, 2013.

Whitehurst, Tess. *The Magic of Trees: A Guide to Their Sacred Wisdom & Metaphysical Properties*. Woodbury, MN: Llewellyn, 2017.

Tess Whitehurst's entire catalogue is inspiring and truly magical. These two encyclopedic books features more than 80 varieties of flowers or trees, their magical properties, and spells and rituals for each one. Whitehurst's books are an amazing blend of practical information and ways to live an absolutely magical life.

# Glossary

**aether/akasha/spirit:** *Aether*, *spirit*, and *akasha* are all names for the fifth element, which is completely nonphysical. *Aether* and *akasha* are used to describe the cosmos and heavenly bodies, and the realm of gods and spirits.

**annual (plant):** An annual is a plant that completes its entire life cycle—sprouting from a seed to producing its own seeds—during a single growing season and then dies.

**aura:** The aura is the metaphysical energy field that surrounds the human body and works in tandem with the chakras. The color, shape, and condition of a person's aura can indicate different elements of their personality or spiritual development.

**biennial:** These are flowering plants that take two years to complete their growing cycle. In the first year, they grow roots, stems, and leaves, and in year two, they produce flowers, fruit, and seeds before dying.

**chakra:** Sanskrit for "wheels," the chakras are points of physical and spiritual energy all throughout your body. There are seven main chakras that correspond with different parts of our bodies and forces like intuition, emotions, or psychic abilities. Each chakra is associated with a color, symbol, organ, and element.

**crystals:** The words *crystal*, *stone*, and *rock* are used interchangeably in witchcraft, though in science there is a difference. Each mineral has its own energy, power, and effects on our physical and metaphysical health.

**element:** The classical Western elements are earth, air/wind, fire, water, and aether or spirit. Each element is aligned with certain energies, behaviors, parts of the body, and activities.

**familiar:** A familiar animal is one that belongs to a witch and assists them in their magical work. Historically, familiars were supernatural entities or spirits, but modern witches often refer to their pets as familiars if they share a spiritual connection.

**folk magic:** Folk magic or folk religion refers to spiritual and cultural practices that originate in a specific place or among a specific group of people. It often exists outside the dominant religion but is practiced alongside it.

**hardiness zone:** The hardiness zone scale categorizes the climate in different areas to rate it for the life and survival of plants. This will tell you what kinds of plants grow naturally, what you can plant outside and what you have to grow indoors, and the length of the growing cycle.

**hedge witch:** This is a type of witch who, like green witches, uses herbal magic and healing but also incorporates more esoteric practices like astral travel and divination. The name comes from the expression "riding the hedge," which meant to have one foot in our world—the living world—and one foot in the world of the dead, faeries, or astral plane.

**herbalist:** An herbalist can harvest and cultivate medicinal herbs, turn them into medicine, and dispense them to patients. This takes years of training and is a highly regulated practice in some places.

hoodoo: Hoodoo is one of many African diasporic religions practiced throughout the Americas, arriving with those traded as slaves from Africa. More of a practice than an entire religion, hoodoo came from the enslaved people concentrated mainly around the Mississippi Delta in the southern United States. It spread all over the United States and Canada, especially in places along the Underground Railroad. Hoodoo incorporates herbs, roots, plants, powders, and other talismans into a magical practice along with Christian belief and stories.

kitchen witch: This type of green witch focuses their magical attention on the home and hearth. The kitchen is the witch's altar space, and their cooking utensils are their magical tools. Many make medicines, magical foods and meals, and practice magic to help their family.

mojo/charm bag: This small bag is a spell that can be carried on the body. Traditional mojo bags, which originated in hoodoo, usually consist of a red flannel bag filled with an uneven number of herbs, roots, crystals, coins, shells, and other talismans.

perennial (plant): This is a plant with a life cycle lasting more than two or three years.

planetary ruler: When a magical item is associated with the energy of a certain planet, that planet is known as its planetary ruler. This is a medieval practice that allows us to categorize the different energies of magical items.

traditional Chinese medicine: This 3,000-year-old system of natural medicine combines the use of medicinal herbs, acupuncture, food therapy, massage, and therapeutic exercise to keep the qi, or life force, in harmony.

# Index

Rosemary, 100
Rose of Jericho, 82
Rose quartz, 147
Rue, 83–84

## S

Sabbats, 35–36
Sacral Healing Bath Salts, 70–71
Sacred Smoke Cleansing Wand, 88–89
Sacred Tree Incense, 130–131
Sacrifice, 7
Sage, 78–79
Samhain (Halloween), 35
Sandalwood, 128
Scissors, 21–22
Sea, 27, 42
Seasons, 35–36
Senses, 47–49
Sequoia (redwood), 123
Sixth sense, 49
Solstices, 35–36
Spirituality, 4–5
Stars, 10–11, 36–37
St. John's wort, 105–106
Stones and crystals, 20–21, 141–143.
    *See specific*
    Aquamarine Crystal Elixir, 156
    Crystal Grid for Courage, 154–155
    Crystal Plant Medicine, 158
    Galaxyite Aura Cleanse, 153
Sun, 10–11, 36–37
Sunflower, 59

## T

Tea plant, 82–83
Technology, 6–7
Tools, 20–23, 25
Tree agate, 144–145
Tree of life, branches of, 18–20
Trees. See Wood and trees
Tropical zodiac, 38, 52
Twine, 22

## V

Values, 8–9
Van Van Oil, 109
Vervain, 106–107

## W

Water element, 45
Weather, 11
Wheel of the Year, 35–36
Wicca, 4
Wilderness, 37, 42
Willow, 124–125, 138
Wisdom, 19
Witch hazel, 85
Wood and trees, 24, 119. *See specific*
    The Ace of Wands, 134–135
    Celtic tree zodiac, 39–41
    If the Broom Fits, Ride It, 132–133
    Maple Syrup Sweetening Spell,
      136–137
    Sacred Tree Incense, 130–131
Workspace, 25
World tree, 24

## Y

Yew, 126
Yule (winter solstice), 35–36

## Z

Zodiac
    Celtic tree, 39–41
    tropical, 38, 52

# Acknowledgments

Thank you so much to the team at Callisto, who helped me achieve one of my biggest dreams.

I would never have made it without my sister, the Scorpio, who kept me sane, supported, and in good spirits. There was never such a devoted sister.

I'm so fortunate to have an online network of incredible witches who inspire me every day. Thanks to the W n' B, who inspires me to keep learning and made it possible for me to be a full-time witch; the authors and artists who've joined me on the podcast or shared their perspectives, like Lasara Firefox Allen (the first!), Lisa Marie Basile, Sarah Potter, Joanna Devoe, Fiona Horne, Lilith Dorsey, and Aliza Einhorn; and every other witch who has encouraged me along the way.

Most of all, big love to all the listeners of *The Fat Feminist Witch Podcast*, who have shown me how magical life can be. You mean the world to me.

# About the Author

**PAIGE VANDERBECK** has been the host of *The Fat Feminist Witch Podcast* since 2015 but rode into witchcraft on the Wiccan wave of the 1990s. Despite being a total Capricorn, she's always entertained the mystical and unbelievable and has made the search for it her life's purpose. She's written and spoken about modern witchcraft, fat acceptance, and feminism on her own website, Medium, Revelist, The Dot, and Flare, and on the *New World Witchery*, *Magick and Mediums*, *Cannabis Act*, and *Hippie Witch* podcasts. She trained as a doula with toLabor in New York City, studied history and humanities at Douglas College in British Columbia, and graduated from the tourism and travel program at St. Clair College in Ontario.

Paige lives in Windsor, Ontario, Canada, with her cat, Clover, a betta named Fish, and a house full of ghosts. Visit her online at TheFatFeministWitch.com.

# NOTES

# NOTES

# NOTES

# NOTES

# NOTES

# NOTES

# NOTES

# NOTES

# NOTES